KNOW
&
GROW

KNOW
&
GROW

Volume 1

by
Cheryl Fawcett

REGULAR BAPTIST PRESS
1300 North Meacham Road
Post Office Box 95500
Schaumburg, Illinois 60195

Library of Congress Cataloging in Publication Data

Fawcett, Cheryl, 1953–
  Know and grow.

  1. Sunday-schools—Exercises, recitations, etc.
I. Title.
BV1570.F38   1982   268'.4   82–21567
ISBN 0–87227–086–6 (v. 1)
ISBN 0–87227–090–4 (v. 2)

©1983
Regular Baptist Press
Schaumburg, Illinois
Printed in U.S.A.
2nd printing—1986

To my eager children and supportive co-workers at Faith Baptist Church, Winfield, Illinois: you encouraged my search for truth in the Book of Books; I am gratefully knowing truth and by it growing.

CONTENTS

Introduction   9
Sample Lesson   11

I HAVE A QUESTION

Can You Please God?   19
What Are You Looking For?   22
Am I Guilty Before God?   26
How Is Sin Paid For?   29
How Does God Save Us?   33
What Was Christ Made for Us?   37
Who Is God's Lamb?   40
Are You Saved for Sure?   43
Are You His Sheep?   46

SIN AND SALVATION

Can I Inherit Eternal Life?   53
What Is Sin?   56
Sin and the Cross   59
By Whose Name?   63
Salvation by the Cross Alone   67
Things Cannot Save You   71
The New Man   75
Conflict of the Old and New   79

WHAT IS GOD LIKE?

What Is God Like?   87
God Is Love   91
God Is Truth   96

God Is Sovereign   100

God Is Holy   104

God Is Just   108

God Is Omnipresent, Omnipotent,
Omniscient   112

God Is Eternal   117

God Is Infinite   121

God Is Immutable   125

SEASONAL SPECIALS

Know the Future (*Halloween*)   131

One Says Thanks (*Thanksgiving*)   135

To Tell the Truth (*Washington's Birthday*)   139

I Can Live for God This Summer
(*Summer*)   144

His Name Is Wonderful (*Christmas*)   147

His Name Is Counselor (*Christmas*)   150

His Name Is the Mighty God (*Christmas*)   154

His Name Is the Everlasting Father
(*Christmas*)   158

His Name Is Prince of Peace (*Christmas*)   162

PREFACE

Bible memorization is a vitally important activity for children. They must know the truth before they can understand and live it daily. They may and often do *know* a Bible text without even a hint as to its relationship or meaning to them.

I became acutely aware of this problem as I led a children's club which majored on memorization. The 30 devotionals contained in these pages grew out of my desire to help our "kids" be more than parrots of Bible verses.

It is written for the teacher who would be a guide for children on the journey from "knowing" through "understanding" to "living and doing" the truth of Scripture.

Each lesson includes specific aims to assist the teacher in achieving the goal of understanding as well as directions for visualizing and applying each text to a child's life experience.

It is my desire that more grade school children will understand and live the truths they so readily commit to memory. Teacher, you are the key and here is a resource to help you.

— *Cheryl Fawcett*

Below is a sample lesson. Each area is explained briefly. Please read this carefully. It reveals much that will be helpful in the teaching of these lessons.

SAMPLE LESSON

Scripture Text: Each lesson begins with a Scriptural base that gives direction and structure. The text is the source of the truths taught. Second Timothy 3:16, 17 explains that "all Scripture is given by inspiration of God, and is profitable . . . That the man of God may be perfect, throughly furnished unto all good works." We see that all of the Bible is from God. Secondly, what He has given to us is for our benefit. The final phrases give two results of the study of God's inspired Word. First, it makes the man of God complete, mature. Second, it completely equips for service. Many of the texts used are key texts and students and teachers will be wise to commit them to memory.

Lesson Aim: The lesson aim is a target for the instructor. It states what the student will be able to do as a result of this lesson. Knowing what you hope to accomplish is a first step in achieving it. There are four qualities that are necessary for an aim. It must be practical (reasonable, so the learner is willing to try), reachable (expect the learner can achieve this), specific (exact enough to know if it is done), and measurable (you will know if it is accomplished). We have attempted to use these guidelines in writing aims for each lesson. The teacher may desire to add aims of his own, using the qualities given above. The key concept is to write aims in terms of what the learner will be able to know, apply and do as a result of the lesson. Study the lesson aim before teaching. After the lesson presentation, review the aim to evaluate the achievement of the learner. This practice will help the teacher to focus the lesson and accomplish more in the student's heart and life.

Are You Ready?

This portion of the lesson is written to the student. It gives one way of introducing the topic to be studied. The teacher must earn the right to teach every time they meet. Each pupil enters the class with a personal set of thoughts, dreams, intentions. Many times the intention of the teacher is much different from that of his pupils because of his prior study and preparation. This is not wasted time; it is necessary. Building a common ground of experience and thought draws the students to consider the lesson. They need time to get ready.

In his book, *Creative Bible Teaching* (Moody Press, 1970), Lawrence Richards states the three hurdles to be crossed in the lesson introduction:

(1) Get attention. Ideally, everyone takes part.
(2) Set a goal. Answer the student's question, "Why should I listen to this?"
(3) Lead naturally into Bible study.

A variety of methods is used both in reviewing previous work and in introducing new topics. Additional help is given in the visual section. Be creative. The approach given may be poor for your group. Devise an approach of your own, using the three steps above. Proceed when the students are ready . . . not before.

See for Yourself

This section of the lesson is directed to students. They are encouraged to open their Bibles. They need to read, answer questions, reason, respond to what they see and learn. Learning is an *active* participative process. The teacher assists the student to find in the text that which the teacher now understands to be true.

It takes patience to walk someone else along a path you have already traveled, but it is a rewarding exercise. There is joy in discovery; allow the pupil this joy.

This section contains background information that is not given directly in the text. This added help will illuminate what the student has already seen for himself.

Don't fall into the trap of *telling* the students all you have learned and found to be true. They will retain much longer and more readily internalize what they see for themselves. You are the guide in a stimulating, exhilarating teaching/learning process. You need to have traveled the trail first in order to be a qualified guide. Carefully, prayerfully lead them in an expedition to unearth the spectacular truths contained in the Bible.

An open Bible is a MUST for student and guide alike. Don't develop that bad habit of guessing or recalling from memory. Go to the text and search out the answer. Find out what it really does say. The Scripture is reliable but your memory may not be.

Live It

This is the response to the truth discovered and learned. It is one thing to know the truth. It is quite another to examine one's life against the truth. It is still another thing to lay definite plans to implement the truth in living.

The student often asks in his mind, "So what! What does all of this mean to me?" This section endeavors to take a first step in suggesting some of the "so whats" of Bible truth.

Response is required. Allow time for thought and decision. This is so closely linked to the previous section that it should appear that they are one and the same. Both are important for complete learning to occur. We must know the truth first; then we must live it.

John 13:17 records Jesus' response-invitation to His disciples. He had just taught them a significant lesson in leadership and serving. He had shown them how to live this and then He challenged them. "If ye know these things, happy are ye if ye do them." The pupils need to be shown and challenged to live the truth.

To the Instructor: Make It Visual

Visualizing your presentation is not optional; it is vital for several reasons. First, to avoid misunderstanding, we need to visualize what we attempt to communicate verbally. Words can mislead, confuse, confound. Words accompanied by pictures or visuals are less likely to do so. Clarity is one reason for using visual helps.

Second, ours is a media age. We are accustomed to being communicated with visually, by touch and by experience. Don't teach in the dimension of the spoken word only. Add to that the eye gate, the sensation of touch, smell, taste. The more senses employed in learning, the more lasting will be the lesson's impact. The truths you teach are eternal—use every method you have available to enrich and add to their impact.

Third, aids to teaching can help the learner to participate and respond. An active learner is a learner who has a changed life. Don't settle for passive, mindless classroom time. Redeem your student's capacity to enter in and be a growing learner by allowing him to make visuals. The ability to transfer from words to pictures is indicative of thought and understanding. Specific instructions, ideas and resources are given in each lesson.

Note: *This material is written as a tool. Use it. Adapt it to fit your situation, pupils, resources. It is the writer's desire to provide a beginning place for the student to learn basic truths from the Bible for himself. The teacher is the guide for the journey. Life is the test tube of reality. Remember the promise of 2 Timothy 3:17 as you teach your pupils. The truth of God, learned, will make them mature, ready to do every good work!*

I Have
a Question

CAN YOU PLEASE GOD?

Scripture Text: *"But to him that worketh not, but believeth on him that justifieth the ungodly, his faith is counted for righteousness" (Rom. 4:5).*

Lesson Aim: The student will understand that God is pleased with his *faith,* not his works. The student will evaluate his life to see if he is trying to please God by works.

Are You Ready?

Jennifer and John wondered just what they might do to please their mom today. John suggested that if he made his bed without being reminded, Mother would surely be surprised and pleased. Jennifer decided that she would do her homework without being told. "Homework is always something Mom and I fuss over after school every day. If I would get started all on my own, Mom would be pleased with me." The Bible tells us about a man who pleased God. His story is told in the first book of the Bible, Genesis. The man is Abraham and Genesis 15:6 tells us that he believed in the Lord and God credited it or counted his belief as right living. He pleased God. Do you want to please God?

See for Yourself

Open your Bible to Romans chapter 4, verse 5. (*Encourage the students to open their Bibles, too. It is important that they see for themselves. Their learning will be longer lasting if you can help them discover what the text says.*) Who is the first "him" referring to? It means any man, every man; it means you. You could exchange the word "him" for your name. Read the verse with your name in place of the first him. What does the verse say about working? We don't need to work. Something will happen even if we don't work. What does work mean? It has the idea of a task or labor to be done. God isn't pleased or satisfied with the things we *do* to please Him. Can you name some things people do to try and please God? (Going to church, giving money to good causes, praying, not doing bad activities, etc.) Do these please God by themselves? No, they don't. Why not? The next phrase will tell us.

What can we do to please God? (*Have the student read it from the verse to you.*) Yes, believe. Who are we to believe? The second "him" the verse refers to is God. It could read this way, "But to every man that worketh not, but believeth on God. . . ." To believe is to put your trust in, to lean on someone. If you believe that a chair can hold you, you sit on it and rest your whole weight on it. God is trustworthy. We can believe Him, that is, lean on Him, trust Him to do what He says He will do.

The verse next describes the One we are to believe. What does it say? He justifieth the ungodly. Who are the ungodly? Is it you? Is it I? Yes, we are all ungodly. "Justifieth" is a difficult word, but it means to declare someone or something right. We are told that God declares or tells ungodly men that they are right. Although the verse doesn't tell us how God does this, it does tell us that we are to believe that He does it. This is exciting! You are ungodly before God, but by believing and not working to do it yourself you can be right and pleasing to God.

The last phrase says it again just so we don't miss the point: that man's faith is counted for righteousness. We know that God is perfect. He would be pleased if we were perfect, but we know from this verse and others (Rom. 3:23) that we are ungodly. God can't be pleased with us as we are. He isn't even pleased when we work or do things to try and please Him. Our work does not count for anything, but our faith does! Hebrews 11:6 tells us again that we must believe God in order to please Him.

Live It

Do you want to please God? Will your work please Him? Will your belief (resting on Him to declare you righteous) please Him? Your faith in God is important. Are you working to please Him or are you trusting what He wants to do for you?

To the Instructor: Make It Visual

It will be helpful for you to display the verse visually because some students will not have Bibles. The visual impact will help them remember the truth taught. Make use of an overhead projector, a chalkboard, even a piece of newsprint. Also, have your Bible handy. The truths you teach are not your ideas alone—the visible Bible tells your students that you,' too, depend on it for the same things you teach them.

WHAT ARE YOU LOOKING FOR?

Scripture Text: *"For the grace of God that bringeth salvation hath appeared to all men, teaching us that, denying ungodliness and worldly lusts, we should live soberly, righteously, and godly, in this present world; Looking for that blessed hope, and the glorious appearing of the great God and our Saviour Jesus Christ" (Titus 2:11–13).*

Lesson Aim: The student will be able to name two items that Christians are to avoid and three ways believers are to live. The student should determine whether he is looking for the return of the Lord Jesus.

Are You Ready?

It was late afternoon. Susan sat near the window in the dining room watching anxiously up the road. Joan came to the front door and asked Susan to come outside and join in a game. "No, thanks," Susan replied, "I am waiting for my grandma and grandpa to arrive. They are coming for dinner. Another time, okay? I really want to be here when they come."

Have you ever waited for a special someone to arrive? If it

was someone you loved and were anxious to see, you may have responded as Susan did. Other activities that were previously important to you don't seem so important as the arrival of someone special draws near. Today we will discuss the arrival of another Person and the changes His arrival will make in the lives of those waiting and watching.

See for Yourself

Open your Bible to the book of Titus. This book is a short letter from Paul to a man named Titus. The letter has some important instructions for Titus and for us as well. Let's look at Titus 2:11 through 13. Read the verses to yourself. What has appeared to all men? Verse 11 tells us that God's grace has appeared to all. Grace means God's favor. God's favor has shined on everyone so that everyone can see it. What does this grace bring? Salvation is brought to *all* who receive the grace of God. God wants everyone to receive His favor or grace. Have you received God's favor? Have you realized that God's grace is for you?

Paul tells Titus there is something we should learn after we have enjoyed God's grace in our own lives. We should be taught and instructed in two ways. Can you name them? One is what we are not to do and the other is what we are to do. We are to say "no" to ungodliness and worldliness. We are to say "yes" to sober, righteous and godly living. Let's list each key word and explain what is meant.

NO

Ungodliness— No respect for God or His matters
Worldly lusts— Strong uncontrolled desire for things of the world

---

YES	
Soberly—	Self-controlled, balanced, temperate (it does not mean a long, sad face!)
Righteously—	Upright, fair, right living
Godly—	Full of respect, reverent—respectful of God

It is important that we are told what not to do, but more important that we are told what we *should* do. Those are hard instructions for us—we will need God's help to live that way. We are told to begin *now*—in this present age. Where is your present world? Does it include your home, your school, your church, your club, the store and your time with friends? Yes, we are not to wait until some other time. We are told to live that way now.

The reason that we should live the way verse 12 explains is revealed in verse 13. Can you see it? We are looking for the appearing, the coming of Someone. This Someone is described and then named. The Person is Jesus Christ. Where is He now? We can be sure that He *is* coming. He is a great God. He is the Savior, the promised One. He is Jesus—the God-Man. We already have His salvation and now as we live soberly, righteously and godly, we look for His appearing.

Live It

Are you looking for the appearing of Jesus? Are you living so you will be ready for Him? If you are frightened that He may come, maybe you need to receive His salvation. If you are not looking for Him, is it because you aren't living as He instructed? His coming is sure. This week, consider how often you think about His return. He will forgive your ungodliness and worldly lusts if you will ask His forgiveness. Do it now and request His help to live soberly, righteously and godly in your present world.

To the Instructor: Make It Visual

The teacher may want to use a magazine picture to gain the initial attention of students and to illustrate the opening story. It would be helpful to write out the verses for an overhead projector, or on a chalkboard, or use newsprint. Encourage students to use their own Bibles. They will need help, but it is important for them to see for themselves that what you teach is indeed true.

AM I GUILTY BEFORE GOD?

Scripture Text: *"Wherefore, as by one man sin entered into the world, and death by sin; and so death passed upon all men, for that all have sinned" (Rom. 5:12).*

Lesson Aim: The student will be able to respond to the lesson's question in the affirmative and to explain that this is because of Adam's sin and his own sin. The student should sense the weight of the guilty verdict in his/her spiritual standing before God.

Are You Ready?

Today's question is important for you to answer. What does "guilty" mean? *(Allow students to respond.)* How do you feel inside when you really are guilty? "Guilty" means, in part, to deserve blame or punishment, to have done something wrong. Some feel sick when they are guilty. Some are embarrassed and feel like everyone is looking at them. Some would like to hide and not look at the one before whom they are guilty. Some want to blame someone else for what they did. Each of us has felt guilty for one reason or another. We may react differently, but the point is that we are guilty and that guilt does affect us.

The Bible tells us about a man named Adam. God had given him a specific instruction and Adam had disobeyed the

26

instruction. He was guilty. How did he respond (Gen. 3:8)? He hid because he didn't want to face God. He blamed his guilt on his wife, Eve. The truth was, Adam, too, was guilty.

See for Yourself

Romans 5:12 talks more about Adam's guilt and how it affects you and me. But you didn't eat the forbidden fruit. You've never even been to the Garden of Eden. Why should Adam's sin affect you? Let's look together and discover the answer.

The verse opens with what word? Yes, it is "wherefore." That is a summary word and it indicates that what follows is a restatement of the preceding paragraph.

How many people are mentioned in the next phrase? One man is mentioned here. "Wherefore, as by Adam. . . ." What happened by this man? Sin entered the world. Picture a stage. It is empty except for Adam and Eve in the perfect garden which God made. Now at the left enters sin. He is dressed in black and is escorted by Adam. Before this there was no sin in the garden or in the world. God made it perfect. By his disobedience Adam brought sin to God's perfect world.

Next is the result of sin's entrance. It is a serious condition. It is as though sin brings a guest along with him. Return to our stage image. Adam brings sin and sin brings with him, death. The two are together. Death is not pretend or fake; he is very real. Adam and Eve both began to die that very instant they allowed sin to enter.

The verse tells us that Adam and Eve aren't the only ones who die. Who is subject to death according to this verse? All men are to die. No one escapes. It is not possible to hide from and avoid death. Blaming someone else will not change the fact that death comes to every person.

Does it seem fair to you that a man, Adam, sinned and you get punished? Our verse answers that thought. It tells us another reason why death passes upon all men. What is the reason? It begins with the word "for." All have sinned, missed the mark, transgressed, broken God's standards. So we follow Adam's pattern. We, too, sin and by so doing we allow death to come upon us.

Notice the contrast here. One man versus all men. Next notice similarities: Adam sinned—we, too, have sinned; Adam died—we, too, die.

Live It

Our question today is, am I guilty before God? On the basis of Romans 5:12, how would you answer? You are guilty before God—you have sinned. What is the penalty for your sin? The verse says that sin brings death. Can you escape death? John 3:16 tells us that God does not want you to die, but to have life.

To the Instructor: Make It Visual

The teacher may seek to display the question for the lesson where it can be visible to students even before the lesson time. Continue to make the verse visual for the study time and encourage all to use Bibles. A visual idea is given below.

HOW IS SIN PAID FOR?

Scripture Text: *"Neither by the blood of goats and calves, but by his own blood he entered in once into the holy place, having obtained eternal redemption for us" (Heb. 9:12).*

Lesson Aim: The student will be able to select the answer to the lesson's question from a given list of options. The student should further be able to explain his answer from the text studied. The student will be encouraged to reflect on his own personal answer to the question, to determine what he is counting on to pay for his sin.

Are You Ready?

(Note: It will be helpful to review lessons one and two with their respective texts and answers. The students should be encouraged to jointly respond as the questions are asked. The explanation of their answers will help the teacher discern what they have learned. Right learning can be reinforced and error corrected. Students don't always learn what we intend. Review is vital and profitable for both teacher and student.)

How is food paid for? Your mom or dad uses money and sometimes coupons, too. Sometimes a check is used. How do you pay for the gas in your family's car? Cash and credit cards are the two most familiar ways to us. What would happen if you attempted to trade a bag of peanuts for a carton of milk? Suppose your father took your baseball card collection to the gas station and tried to make a trade for a gallon or two? The peanuts and the baseball cards are both valuable and even useful, but they don't serve in the same way as money. Today's question is similar. How is sin paid for? Some of the answers young people and adults give to that question are as silly and confused as trying to buy gas with baseball cards. Let's examine Hebrews 9:12 for the answer God wants us to know.

See for Yourself

Give another term for the opening word of verse 12. "Not even," "never" and "no" are all possible answers. We find here first of all what won't work. We are told how not to answer the question. The blood of goats and calves will not pay for sin.

Hebrews was written to a group of Jewish people. The Jews had been God's special people for a long time. They had specific instructions on how to worship God and what to do when they committed sin. The instructions are recorded in the Old Testament. They had been told to bring a goat (Lev. 4:23) or a bull (Lev. 4:3) as a sin offering. Now they are being told that they are not to bring these animals any longer. The reason for this new arrangement follows next.

"But" stands out in strong contrast. It tells us that what went before (blood of animals) and what follows are not the same. What does follow and is in place of the blood of animals? Yes, it is His own blood. Verse 11 tells you Whose blood is referred to. Name Him. Christ is the Person Who offers blood. It is *His* blood, not someone else's. It is not the blood of an animal but the blood of the God-Man.

His blood is important, for when a man gives his blood he gives his life. Yes, Christ's blood was given and so was His life. He died on the cross for the Hebrews and for us, too.

What He did with His blood is also important. Can you discover from the verse where He went with His blood? He went into the holy place. How many times did He enter there? Once and only once (Heb. 9:12). The word "entered" has the idea of a specific time and place. In other words, it is a fact of history that Christ went to the holy place—a once-for-all journey. Never again will it be necessary for Him to repeat this.

Just what is this holy place? In verses 1 through 11 you will find a description of the place to which the Hebrews took the blood of their animal sacrifices. It was called a tabernacle. It was a portable worship building. The holy place was the innermost room where the blood of the animal was to be poured on the top of a special piece of furniture. We know that it was a real place and of special significance in their relationship to God. Verse 11 states that Christ entered another tabernacle, similar to the first in that it is real and a holy place. It is different in that it is not a building. It was not made with hands. We believe that this place is Heaven. It is a real place and is most holy since God is there.

Why did Christ go to the holy place with His blood? The final phrase tells us. He obtained eternal redemption for us. As He entered, He paid an eternal or never-ending price for the Hebrew believers and for us; in other words, He redeemed us. Redemption means that He rescued us from the penalty of sin. Sin must be paid for, and He paid for sin with His own blood.

Live It

The sacrifice of animals was repeated as often as sin was committed. Christ's sacrifice was made *once!* What a contrast. His payment for sin was once, forever!

From this list, select which can pay for sin. Explain your choice.

_____ Good works

_____ Prayers

_____ Blood of bulls

_____ Blood of goats

_____ Blood of Christ

What are you counting on to pay for your sin? You probably don't make animal sacrifices, but you may do other things to try to pay for your sin. Christ's blood did pay for your sin. Will you try to bring your "peanuts" or "baseball cards" to do it, or will you accept His work for you?

To the Instructor: Make It Visual

Give assistance to the students who are not yet adept at handling the Word of God. They need to learn to find in the Word the same things you have discovered. It is an open book. The Lord intends for us to not only teach its contents but also to find in it the answers to life's questions. Seize upon their eagerness to read and see and think.

It would be helpful to have a chart or diagram of the tabernacle as you explain the holy place. You may prepare ballots to distribute at the conclusion. Ask each pupil to respond to the questions given above. It will be valuable for each to realize his decision is just that—his decision.

HOW DOES GOD SAVE US?

Scripture Text: *"Not by works of righteousness which we have done, but according to his mercy he saved us, by the washing of regeneration, and renewing of the Holy Ghost" (Titus 3:5).*

Lesson Aim: The student will be able to name washing and renewing as the "how" of God saving us.

Are You Ready?

Today's lesson has a very specific focus. It does not ask who saves us. It does not ask when, where or even why God saves us. Those questions are all important but they are not in focus today. We are asking "how?" The aim is to determine the means or method used to bring us to Christ.

When Eric Heiden skated to victory in the 1980 Winter Olympics, winning five gold medals, many spectators were asking "how?" How does he do this? How can he do it so well and with such consistency? News stories centered on the "how" of Eric Hciden's amazing accomplishment. They revealed his hard work in training, his determination to excel and his dogged persistence when there were other activities he could have spent his time on. Each of these answers the question "how?"

As we examine Titus 3:5, we will discover the "how" of God's saving us. Are you ready?

33

See for Yourself

Open your Bible and fill in the missing key words from Titus 3:5. (*See visual helps.*) When you have finished, circle the word in the middle of the verse that tells you a contrast is given here. If you circled the word "but" you were correct.

The opening phrase helps us to understand something that is often confused. Most of the people on your street would answer today's question beginning with the second word of the first phrase. They would tell you, "By works of righteousness which we have done we will be saved." What kinds of works of righteousness or right living do they have in mind? Name several. (Go to church, give money to charity, visit sick, read the Bible, say prayers, love my neighbor.) According to Titus 3:5, will those things save them? Why or why not?

No, they won't. The verse says, "Not by. . . ." There are two things wrong with the answer "My work will save me." First of all, the wrong person is at work. Who does the work of salvation? The verse says He, God, saves us. We see further that salvation is not earned but is given on the basis of His mercy. "Mercy" means pity, compassion, or kindness; He withholds punishment that we rightfully deserve. It is not our work piled up high enough to please Him. We could never earn His salvation (Matt. 16:26). Rather, He has mercy on us.

Next comes a key word—"by." It tells us the answer to the "why" question that follows. It has two parts. Can you name them? The first is the washing of regeneration and the second, the renewing of the Holy Ghost. Now, what do they mean?

The word "washing" has the idea of a bath, not just a sponge-bath or washcloth cleansing, but a complete washing. This is a picture of our salvation. God does not get us into the bathtub and give us a literal scrubbing. We do know, though, that to Him we are unclean ones (Isa. 64:6). He does desire us to be clean, and through His "washing" we are made clean (John 15:3). This washing is specific and special. It is the washing of regeneration, and cleansing of the new birth. His washing makes us new—clean from sin and clean before the Father.

The second word, "renewing," means renovation, new, freshness. Have you ever been to an old building that was renovated? What was done to it? It was made to look like new inside—refreshed, repainted, cleaned up, refurnished and made over. Our text tells us Who does the renovation in the one being saved; the Holy Spirit. Yes, the Holy Spirit not only renews the person, He moves right in to take charge of the work. The Holy Spirit gives Himself to everyone who is saved. He lives inside and sees to it that the renewing is completed.

Live It

How does God save us? Two ways—first of all by washing away the sin we have and, secondly, by renewing us through the Holy Ghost. Have you been cleansed by God's mercy? If you have, will you thank Him for His mercy towards you? If you haven't, why not let Him wash you today from all your sin? The Holy Spirit is renewing you if you are cleansed. Are you cooperating with His work—yielding every area to His

control—or are you resisting His renewing and wondering why you are not happy?

To the Instructor: Make It Visual

Give each student a copy of the verse to be studied. Insert blanks in place of the following words and have them fill in the blanks with the proper words: works, righteousness, according, mercy, washing, regeneration, renewing, Holy Ghost. This paper and pencil activity will assist the students in getting the message for themselves. The suggested visual on page 35 to summarize and visualize the truth taught would be useful.

WHAT WAS CHRIST MADE FOR US?

Scripture Text: *"For he hath made him to be sin for us, who knew no sin; that we might be made the righteousness of God in him" (2 Cor. 5:21).*

Lesson Aim: The student will be able to answer the lesson's question. Christ was made sin for us. Because He was declared guilty before God, we are made righteous.

Are You Ready?

The story of the "Prince and the Pauper" tells of two young men who looked very much alike. They exchanged clothes and places to explore the world of the other. Taking the place of another can be fun, revealing, fearsome and even dangerous.

Our lesson today involves an exchange. It is a bit difficult, but with your best thinking and effort I am sure you will understand.

See for Yourself

As you are opening your Bibles to 2 Corinthians 5:21, please be reminded of our question for today: What was Christ made for us? Let's begin by reading the text out loud twice. *(This will help familiarize the students with the entire scope before zeroing in on the particulars.)*

Did you notice that words like he, him and us appear

repeatedly? If we can discover who these persons are, we will be on the way to understanding the direction of the verse.

There are three distinct persons involved. Can you give their identifications from the verse?

1. He—the One Who makes Him to be sin.
2. Him—the One Who is made to be sin.
3. Us—the Christians at Corinth.

Verse 20 will give a clue as to the identity of the first Person. Can you figure it out? He is God. God is the Person Who makes Someone to be sin for us. The second Person is described further on in verse 21, where it says He knew no sin. This Person was not acquainted with sin. He had never sinned and was perfect before the Father. Who is He? Jesus Christ was without sin. He fits the description given.

Replace the names for the pronouns and read: "For God hath made Jesus to be sin for the Corinthians, who knew no sin, that the Corinthian believers might be made the righteousness of God in Jesus."

Jesus was made to be sin, or to be guilty, on behalf of men who were sinners. It is impossible for us to realize what that means. We know sin, we live in sin, we practice sin daily. But Jesus was perfect, without sin. Originally this verse was written to a group of sinners at Corinth, but the truth of it applies to us today as well. He was made to be sin for our sake, on our behalf.

The exchange is not complete without the end of the verse. We are made something, too. What is it? We are made the righteousness of God in Jesus. Now, that sounds really great. But what is righteousness? It means innocence or holiness. What an exchange! We are made holy or innocent before God and Jesus is made to be sin, or guilty, for us.

Live It

Are you holy? Are you innocent of all wrong? Is Jesus perfect, holy before God? Yes, He is without sin and we are guilty of sin and breaking God's law. On the basis of 2

38

Corinthians 5:21, what exchange takes place? Have you had that exchange in your life? Do you stand holy, innocent before the Father? Or are you still carrying your weight of sin? Christ is willing to take your sin and give you His righteousness.

To the Instructor: Make It Visual

It would be helpful to have the verse displayed in the teaching area. As different words are referred to they may be pointed out, circled, underlined, starred or whatever means you might want to use.

You might desire to visualize the exchange made by labeling a large, dark bag "sin" and a clean, white robe or sheet of tag board "holy." The instructor can then exchange his sin for righteousness. He should probably leave the room carrying the sin burden and return wearing the robe.

The verse may be diagramed in the following manner:

When using a diagram, reveal only one line at a time. This will help build suspense and keep your students with you, not ahead or daydreaming.

WHO IS GOD'S LAMB?

Scripture Text: *"Behold the Lamb of God, which taketh away the sin of the world" (John 1:29).*

Lesson Aim: The student will be able to answer the question with the name of Jesus. The student should be able to explain to the instructor that Jesus was a sacrificial Lamb—given for our sins.

Are You Ready?

Can you identify this tune? *(Play "Mary Had a Little Lamb" on the piano.)* We all know it to be—*(allow students to answer).* Listen carefully as some different words are given to this song you all know. Ready? *(Sing.)* Mary had a little lamb *(repeat "little lamb" twice)*, Mary had a little lamb *(pause),* she laid Him in a manger. That answers today's question in sort of a riddle.

See for Yourself

Can anyone tell me what lambs were used for in the Old Testament? They were used as a sacrifice for sin, and they were used for food, and their wool was used to make clothing.

Today we are talking about a special Lamb. This Lamb gave Himself for us. He was innocent, but He patiently endured the awful process of being offered as a sin sacrifice.

Turn in your Bible to John 1:29. John the Baptist was talking about Someone coming soon. Notice verse 15—"He that cometh after me . . ." and verse 27—". . . who coming after me is preferred before me." John was talking about the soon arrival of this Lamb of God.

In verses 21 and 22, priests and Levites came and asked John who he was. He answered in verse 23, "I am the voice of one crying in the wilderness." John was looking for Someone else. It wasn't important who he, John, was. In verse 29 we find the arrival of the One John awaited.

The opening word has the element of surprise. John was excited—he spoke strongly as he said, "Behold." Look, he is saying, this is absolutely necessary, urgent. For a long time John had told others that this One was coming, and now there He was! It is possible to imagine John shouting out, "Hey, look, don't miss this, it is important!"

The next four words tell us the title of this One we are not to miss. Who is He? He is the Lamb of God. Many lambs had been brought *to* God, but this was God's Lamb. He was *from* God. He had come to the world even as John had promised.

What would this Lamb do? He would take away the sin of the world. The words "take away" mean to lift, to carry, to loose and go away with. It is as though we are carrying a heavy load and He comes along to lift the load of sin off us and carry it away.

Whose sin does He carry away? The verse says the sin of the world. It means the sin of all of the inhabitants of the world.

We know the Lamb has arrived and we know what He does. Who is He? Examine the beginning of verse 29. John tells us that Jesus is the Lamb of God. No mistake—in verse 30 he verifies that this was the One he was looking for. "This is He!"

Live It

Who is God's Lamb? Jesus is God's Lamb come to take

away the sin of the world's inhabitants. Why should we behold Him? (1) To see Him—to know Him; (2) to know what He does with sin; (3) to know He wants to take away *our* sin.

To the Instructor: Make It Visual

The instructor may desire to pantomime the verse for the class. It is easily done and will draw every student's attention. First, point to all the class. Second, point to eyes, making a motion for looking or seeing. Third, have a helper enter carrying a heavy sack (*dark trash bag filled with newspaper works well*) over his shoulder. Instructor motions to traveler his willingness to carry the load. The traveler first refuses, then agrees. The load is transferred and both exit. Give students an opportunity to talk about what they observed. This will reinforce learning and increase attention.

Another suggestion is to write the verse on a roll of shelf paper. As you proceed, reveal each line. Sketch below:

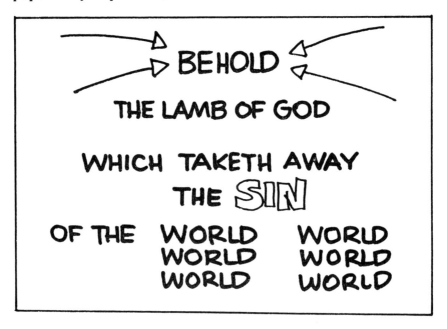

ARE YOU SAVED FOR SURE?

Scripture Text: *"For whosoever shall call upon the name of the Lord shall be saved" (Rom. 10:13).*

Lesson Aim: The student should evaluate if he or she has urgently called upon the Lord and thus experienced saving faith.

Are You Ready?

The question today is important for each of us to consider. There are some questions that you may not know the answers to and need not be concerned about. Take this question for example: Are you going to make the school soccer team? You answer I hope so, I think so, I am trying to. Those are appropriate answers. There are some factors you don't know for sure. That causes the answer to be in doubt.

Are you saved for sure? This question needs a firm answer. You shouldn't "hope so," "think so" or "try to"—you should *know*. The verse we study today will tell you what you need to know in order to answer. Your response will affect your life and your future.

See for Yourself

After you open the Bible to Romans 10:13, we will all read the verse out loud. The apostle Paul was writing to a church in the capital city of Rome. He takes time out, however, to write about his own people, the Jews. We find the account of their present condition at the end of chapter 9 and in all of chapter 10. Romans 10:1 reveals what Paul was wanting and praying for them. What was it? He wanted them to be saved.

In verse 3, something they did not know caused them to be wrong in their efforts to please God. What did they not know? God's righteousness was hidden from them. They were trying to establish their own righteousness by the law God had given them. Does Paul have much hope for them in establishing their own (v. 5)? It is implied that they will never make it.

Paul presents righteousness of faith (not doing for yourself but receiving Christ's work for yourself) as their only hope (vv. 6–8). As we read through this passage, Paul seems to be speaking more and more strongly.

Verse 13 is the last verse of this opening paragraph. It opens with the word "whosoever." Are you in that whosoever? Am I included there? Verse 12 tells us that Jews and Greeks are all included. We could substitute the word "everyone" or "all" for whosoever. Paul is specifically concerned about his relatives, but he strongly states that this salvation is for ALL!

What must be done? The action verb "call" carries with it the voice of urgency. It is the kind of call you give when you are hurt or in trouble and want help quickly. It's not the kind of call that is "just checking" to see if mom or a playmate is still nearby. This call is from an individual who desperately wants a response to the call. Many folks call God's name. Some do so lightly, for a joke, to be funny in front of friends. God knows why we call and He responds when we call in urgency for His saving grace.

Whom do we call upon? We are to call upon the name of the Lord. A name is a symbol of sorts. It represents all that the bearer is in His character and all He does. When we call the name of the Lord Jehovah, we call upon the One Who has all authority, the great Creator and Sustainer of men and women.

In using His name reverently, we call to mind all He is and has done for us through Christ on the cross and in the empty tomb!

If we call, will He answer? The verse says "Whosoever shall call . . . shall be saved." "Shall" is positive and sure. It is a promise that rests on the integrity of God. When you call, He will hear and WILL save you.

What does it mean to be saved? That word is confusing to many. We often use it and figure that everyone knows what it means. It means to rescue or protect. We are in sin and cannot get ourselves free. In saving us He protects us from Satan and his attacks. Satan cannot touch any saved person without God's permission. Thus, you are safe in Him.

Live It

Have you called upon the name of the Lord? Oh, you say, I've always been a Christian. This verse says you aren't until you call upon the name of the Lord. If you have called, this verse is a promise to you. You are His for sure. His ear is open to your call. Today is the day for you to call; tomorrow may be too late.

To the Instructor: Make It Visual

You may desire to make cards for each key word discussed today and display each as you come to it. Poster board will work nicely and you may use the chalkboard or overhead projector. Don't expect children to listen just because you are talking. You may need to earn their attention. Words to include: whosoever, call, name of the Lord, shall, saved.

ARE YOU HIS SHEEP?

Scripture Text: *"My sheep hear my voice, and I know them, and they follow me: And I give unto them eternal life; and they shall never perish, neither shall any man pluck them out of my hand. My Father, which gave them me, is greater than all; and no man is able to pluck them out of my Father's hand. I and my Father are one" (John 10:27–30).*

Lesson Aim: The student on the basis of the description given shall determine whether or not he is one of the Father's sheep. The student should develop a desire to be one of His sheep as a result of knowing the description.

Are You Ready?

What do you know about sheep? *(Allow time for student response.)* They are animals. They are good for food. They provide wool for clothing. They live in large groups and are cared for by a shepherd. They are dumb. Have you ever seen sheep in a circus? They are easily led the wrong way.

In today's lesson, Jesus is talking about sheep. He identifies some as His own. By following along in your Bible, you will be able to know if you are one of His sheep. Not all sheep are His, you know.

See for Yourself

Follow along as we read from John chapter 10, beginning with verse 22 (*read through verse 31*). Let's set the scene for this discussion. Where does this take place (vv. 22, 23)? The setting is the city of Jerusalem in Israel and the temple of Solomon. In other words, this was a religious city and the place of worship. Verse 22 also tells us that this was a religious holiday—the Feast of Dedication.

Surely those gathered in the holy city in this holy place for this holy day would be holy men. Surely they would be men of God. The verses tell us another story about them.

What questions did they ask Jesus? In verse 24 they accused Jesus of causing them to be confused. Their question was: Are you Christ—the One sent from God? What was His response? He tells them in verse 25 that He had already answered their question and they did not believe Him. Not only had He told them, but His works were further proof of the truth of His claim.

The familiar words found in verses 27–30 are Jesus' explanation of why these men didn't receive the truth that Jesus was the One sent from God. They formed a contrast between those who believed and those who were still doubting. Today we, too, fall into one or the other of these groups.

Note: this would be an ideal place in the lesson to fill in the chart shown on page 49.

Just a word of explanation about the sheep of Jesus. He tells us that they hear Him. It is common practice for a shepherd to call to his sheep, and his sheep will respond only to his voice. Other sheep might be within the sound of the shepherd's voice, but will not respond because he is not their shepherd. It is as though they don't hear his voice.

Many shepherds have names for their sheep. They know each one personally. The shepherd knows the personality, health history and temperament of each sheep. He must care for each one of them. They spend many hours together in quiet, lonely places. The shepherd knows his sheep in a variety of ways and uses all of that knowledge to care for them.

Sheep are often kept at night in the safety of a fold. It is a stone walled area and the shepherd sleeps in the doorway. He is the door—no sheep can leave without his knowledge. Often more than one flock spends the night in a single fold. In the morning, each shepherd calls to his sheep (they know his voice) and they fall into line and follow him without question or hesitation. Each shepherd gets his own sheep this way—others will not hear the call or follow.

"I give them eternal life," Jesus told these men. Without the care of the shepherd the sheep will perish or die. This One sent from God delivers them from destruction.

The sheep of the Lord Jesus are safe in His hand. No one can pluck, steal or kidnap them from Him. Being a sheep is dangerous, for there are many enemies. But in the care of the Lord Jesus, they are forever safe and protected.

Live It

Have you heard His voice? The Lord Jesus is calling you to salvation. Or are you playing deaf? Are you pretending His call is for someone else?

Does the Lord Jesus know you? If you are His sheep, He knows everything about you. He knows how to care for you, to feed you, to protect you. Or will He say to you someday, "Depart from me, I never knew you." You should either thank Him for knowing you or ask Him to be your Savior.

Are you following Him? To follow means to be in the same path with someone. Are you in obedience to Him? The Bible has much to say about walking His way. Are you doing what you know to do? If not, maybe you aren't His.

Have you received eternal life? If you are His sheep, you already have it! If not, you will die without Him, outside His protection. You are the target of many enemies.

Take a few minutes now to think about whether or not you are His sheep. Remember, the men Jesus was speaking to were religious. They were even in a place of worship. Yet they did not believe Jesus when He told them Who He really was. How did you respond today?

If you are His, give thanks and be glad. You have much for which to be thankful. If you find that you aren't His, you may call upon the Lord today.

To the Instructor: Make It Visual

The teacher will want to display the chart of comparison. Use whatever available materials you have. Poster board, overhead, chalkboard, newsprint or bulletin board are all possibilities. The outline is given below. Fill in as you go through the lesson.

PLACE:
QUESTION:
ANSWER:

MY SHEEP	UNBELIEVING JEWS

My Sheep	Unbelieving Jews
Hear My voice	Don't hear
I know them	I don't know them
Follow Christ	Don't follow
Have eternal life	Will perish
Safe in Father's hand	Are not in safety of Father's care

Sin
&
Salvation

CAN I INHERIT ETERNAL LIFE?

Scripture Text: *". . . Good Master, what shall I do that I may inherit eternal life?" (Mark 10:17).*

Lesson Aim: The student will be able to name the three wrong assumptions in the rich young man's question, namely: (1) It is not you at work but God. (2) There is nothing you can do. (3) Eternal life is not inherited—it is a free gift to all who receive it.

Are You Ready?

How many times have you done this? You have gone shopping and spotted some item you really liked. However, after checking the price tag, you decided it was too expensive. At that point, you may have determined that the color wasn't just right, the design wasn't exactly what you wanted. The real issue was that it cost too much and you weren't willing to pay that amount for what you would get.

Our study today considers such a situation. A young man examines a price tag and concludes it is too high. He walks away. As far as we know, he did not return. He was in search of eternal life. Let's join the narrative recorded in Mark 10.

See for Yourself

We join the trail of events beginning at verse 17. Jesus and the disciples were on the move. They had paused for a discussion with the Pharisees (vv. 2–12) and for a session with the children (vv. 13–16). As they began to move along, a young man came running up to Jesus.

Yes, he was running. Evidently, he really wanted to talk with Jesus and didn't want Him to get too far before he could ask his question. He was serious about getting an answer to a very specific inquiry.

What did he do next? The text records that he knelt down. What does that tell you about him? It reflects his respect for Jesus. The young man was aware that Jesus was a man of authority. We learn from Luke 18:18 that this man was himself a ruler, yet he showed humility as he bowed before Jesus. Evidently his request was genuine and sincere.

What was the young man's question? *(Allow the students to read it directly from the Bible and then to rephrase it in their own words.)* "Good Master, what shall I do that I may inherit eternal life?" There was something he desired. What was it? He asked about eternal life. He wanted to live forever, not to die. That is an interesting request from a young man. He was aware that he would not be young forever and he was concerned about the life that goes beyond death.

There are three things wrong with his question. Let's talk about them one at a time. First, he asked what may *I* do? He thought that the matter of eternal life was within his ability to do something. Is that true? Can we do anything in ourselves regarding eternal life? Ephesians 2:1 tells us that we are dead in our sins. Dead men can't do anything and neither could this young man. His spirit was not alive; it was dead. So he didn't have eternal life. Someone else would have to care for his need. The question is not what can *I* do, but what will the Lord do for me?

Second, he asks what he could *do*. Jesus answered that he should keep all the commandments. He responded that he had kept them since his youth. Jesus gave him one more command. It was to sell everything he had and then come and follow Jesus. If he would do that he would reveal that his highest love was for Jesus. He must love Jesus more than the things that he had. Was he willing to do this? How do you know? Verse 22 shares that he was sad and went away. Jesus was revealing to him that he really didn't love the Lord with all his heart, soul and mind (Matt. 22:37). We are told in James 2:10 that if we are guilty of the law in one point (he was guilty of having another love), we are guilty of all.

In order to do anything for eternal life we must be without any guilt. That is not possible and so the young man could not do anything.

Thirdly, he implied that eternal life can be inherited. Money may be inherited, that is, passed on to an heir. An official position possibly much like the one this man held could be transferred to an heir. But eternal life must come to everyone directly from God. It cannot be passed on to another.

Live It

Are you like the rich ruler? Are you trying to do for yourself what only God can do for you? Are you trying to keep the law to earn eternal life? If you are guilty in one part you will be guilty of all. In yourself you cannot do what is necessary for eternal life. The commandments were given to help you realize just how far short you are. Flee to Christ and receive His righteousness (2 Cor. 5:21).

You cannot inherit eternal life. Just because your mom, dad, sister, brother, friend, teacher or pastor have eternal life does not mean you have it. You must come directly to God.

To the Instructor: Make It Visual

It will be helpful to outline the three points made for inspection as you progress through the lesson. A teaching picture of the event told here will aid the student in visualizing the rich young ruler.

To catch attention you may want to display several price tags (greatly enlarged for easy observation) attached to a variety of items available to you.

WHAT IS SIN?

Scripture Text: *"For all have sinned, and come short of the glory of God" (Rom. 3:23).*

Lesson Aim: The student will be able to recite the definition of sin. Sin is missing the mark, overstepping God's law.

Are You Ready?

How many of you have ever run in a race? Did you win a prize? What place did you finish in? A race is exciting. Each runner hopes to win and earn a ribbon plus points for his team. Not everyone is given a ribbon. Some fall short—oh, yes, they run the race but not well enough to be rewarded. We call those runners the "also rans." Their names don't make headlines. They aren't in the pictures. They have fallen short of the desired goal. Some "also rans" may do much better than others but none are given ribbons. They all fall short. It doesn't matter how much they fall short, they just don't make it.

Today we are going to study about sin. Hopefully, each of us will learn a simple definition and learn what the Bible says about sin.

See for Yourself

We will be looking closely at Romans 3:23. It is most

likely a familiar passage to you. Listen carefully and see if you can understand something in a new way.

"Sin" is a word that isn't very popular in our modern world. Adults and children alike are hesitant to admit that they have sinned. We use other words which don't sound so bad. Tell me some of these words (mistake, a miscalculation, a small error, a slip-up, a disease, hang-up, etc.).

Our verse tells us how many are involved in this problem of sin. What word lets you know that? The word "all" includes everyone, the whole lot of us. Can anyone exclude themselves from this "all"? No, we are all named here.

Here is a very simple definition for sin. It ties in with our description of running a race. Sin is missing the mark, overstepping God's law. God has given us His standards for our lives. We call these standards His law. When we overstep or disobey that law we have sinned. God also tells us what we are to do—that is, He gives us commands such as honor your parents and love God above all else. When we fail to accomplish these commands we miss the mark, we have sinned. No matter how well we have done, if we fall short in one area we are guilty of sin (James 2:10).

What have we also done in regard to the glory of God? We have fallen short. What is God's glory? It is His dignity, His honor, His praise, His worship. We will never measure up to Him. He is God and we are sinful. God's standard is Jesus Christ, the sinless, perfect Son of God. He measures up to God's glory.

Live It

How do we measure up? If we were to place you on God's standard, how far would you come? Are you short of God's glory? Yes, you say, but so-and-so is even lower than I am. The question is not where so-and-so is but where *you* are.

Remember the illustration of the race. You didn't receive a prize if you fell short of the necessary time. Whether you were one second or ten minutes late, you *fell short*. Likewise, we all fall short of God's glory. As sinners, none of us will share in the prize of Heaven and eternal life.

That's as far as Romans 3:23 takes us. But Romans 6:23 tells the rest of the gospel's good news. Yes, we are all in sin and we deserve not the prize, but the punishment of God. However, there is hope for us, for ". . . the gift of God is eternal life through Jesus Christ our Lord."

Let's repeat the definition of sin: Sin is missing the mark, overstepping God's law.

To the Instructor: Make It Visual

A series of overhead transparencies from Moody Press is available which colorfully illustrates the definition of sin. It is *Basic Bible Doctrine #1, Sin and Salvation,* and is available through Christian bookstores. The series is written and illustrated by Joe Ragont. Overheads 1 and 1A are most helpful in this lesson.

You may also choose other methods of visualizing and displaying the definition of sin to be taught today. Take frequent opportunity to review with your students.

SIN AND THE CROSS

Scripture Text: *"And when they were come to the place, which is called Calvary, there they crucified him, and the malefactors, one on the right hand, and the other on the left. Then said Jesus, Father, forgive them; for they know not what they do. And they parted his raiment, and cast lots. . . . And one of the malefactors which were hanged railed on him, saying, If thou be Christ, save thyself and us. But the other answering rebuked him, saying, Dost not thou fear God, seeing thou art in the same condemnation? And we indeed justly; for we receive the due reward of our deeds: but this man hath done nothing amiss. And he said unto Jesus, Lord, remember me when thou comest into thy kingdom. And Jesus said unto him, Verily I say unto thee, Today shalt thou be with me in paradise" (Luke 23:33, 34; 39-43).*

Lesson Aim: The student will retell the two responses to Christ and the cross: repentance—transfer of sin; or, rejection—retention of sin.

Are You Ready?

What was the question of the rich young ruler? What was

wrong with his question? What is God's standard? Do we measure up? Why? (*See page 54.*)

Today we will discuss a familiar symbol—the cross. Its significance is quite different today than when it was first used by the Romans. In our day, it is a religious symbol, reminding us of the death of Jesus. However, the cross was designed as an instrument of death. It was a cruel punishment reserved for the worst of criminals—Roman citizens were exempted from such means of death. Convicts were fastened on a vertical stake, their hands tied to a crossbar. To die on a cross was a curse (Gal. 3:13), it was painful, it was a despised means of death. We will learn why the cross is today a precious reminder to the believer in Christ.

See for Yourself

Open your Bible to the Old Testament book of Leviticus, chapter 1. Read with me the first few verses, looking for the kind of sacrifice for sin that was commanded by God. An animal of the flock was to be brought. The offering was to be voluntary. Verse 5 tells us that the animal was to be killed and blood offered as a sacrifice for the man who brought it. This was only a temporary arrangement and was to be repeated for every offense. Hebrews 10:4 informs us that this blood sacrifice could not take away sin. It did temporarily cover sin, but was ineffective to take care of it permanently.

Jesus, by His death and the offering of His blood, became a *permanent* Sacrifice to take away our sin. Hebrews 10:10–12 recounts that the priests daily offered sacrifices that could only cover and never take away sin. But Jesus, in *His* sacrifice on the cross, once forever took away sin.

Open your Bible now to Luke chapter 23. This chapter records the crucifixion of Christ. Begin at verse 33 and read who else was put to death that day. Who were they? The Scripture calls them malefactors—they were two criminals, condemned to death.

Skip down to verse 39 and describe the reaction of the

first criminal to Jesus. The verse says he railed or hurled abuse. He was angry and was throwing cruel words at Christ, mocking Him for being in the same situation. He was disrespectful and evidently was not convinced that this was the Christ.

Verses 40 and 41 give the reaction of the second criminal. Tell me what you find there. He did not agree with the first man—he rebuked him. He admitted that he and the other criminal were getting what they deserved. They had committed wrong and were being rewarded fairly. He also claimed that Jesus had done no wrong, yet He was being put to death.

The first man rejected the Person of Christ—he made fun of Him. He also rejected the meaning of Christ's death, so he died carrying his sin with him. The second man realized that Jesus was dying for a purpose. In verse 42 he made an urgent request.

Tell me what he asked Jesus to do for him. He asked Jesus to remember him in His kingdom. He admitted Jesus was God; He addressed Him as Lord. Then the second man asked Jesus to recollect and reward him in that future day.

Does Jesus grant his request? Look at verse 43. Yes! That very day he would be with Him in the place of happiness! Imagine a criminal who realizes Who Jesus is and what His death means, and is forgiven and promised future blessing.

Live It

Just as the two criminals reacted differently to Christ and His death, so do people react differently today. Some mock Christ and will not believe that His death means anything for their sins. In doing so, they die without forgiveness, bearing their own sins.

Others see the death of Christ and have a change of heart. We use the word "repent" but it means the same. By admitting that Jesus is Lord and asking for His forgiveness, they transfer their sin to Him. His death takes away their sin and they are sure of a place in paradise.

Which man are you like? Do you make fun and laugh at talk of the cross and the death of Jesus? Many do so and refuse to be forgiven. You may repent (change your heart) and receive His finished sacrifice to take away your sin.

To the Instructor: Make It Visual

The Moody Press *Basic Bible Doctrine* has an excellent set of visuals for this lesson. Check lesson 2 for further explanation.

BY WHOSE NAME?

Scripture Text: *"Neither is there salvation in any other: for there is none other name under heaven given among men, whereby we must be saved" (Acts 4:12).*

Lesson Aim: The student should be able to give the name by Whom we are saved—Jesus Christ. The student should explain that His name carries with it the authority of God.

Are You Ready?

Picture the following series of events. A massive tractor trailer truck, carrying a heavy load, is coming down a very steep hill. It gains speed as it heads toward its destination just over the next ridge. The driver is counting on gaining good speed going down this hill to help carry him up the incline before him.

At the bottom of the hill stands a very small man. He has a uniform on, is wearing a hat with a star on it, and has his hand held up indicating to the truck driver to stop. Now there is no question about who is larger and carries more weight. Yet the driver applies the brakes and brings the huge rig to a halt just in front of the police officer.

The truck is larger and no match physically for the policeman. There is a difference, however. The policeman can make the truck stop "in the name of the law." The law is more influential than the policeman who represents it. He stands there in the name of the law.

Two men in the book of Acts did amazing miracles, using the name of Someone else Who has great authority.

See for Yourself

The account begins in Acts 3:1. Let's read together through verse 9. Here we find three men involved in a miraculous healing. Who are they? Peter and John were going to pray at the temple when a man who couldn't walk caught their attention. He had never walked, verse 2 tells us, and he was now above 40 years old (Acts 4:22). He had been lame from birth.

Check verse 6 carefully to see in Whose name Peter told him he could walk. "In the name of Jesus Christ of Nazareth rise up and walk." Peter in himself couldn't make the man walk, but only in the name of Jesus. The man took Peter's hand and leaped up. Remember, he had never learned to walk, and here he is leaping and walking.

Chapter 4 verse 2 will give you insight as to how the religious leaders reacted to this miracle and Peter's explanation of it. They were greatly disturbed and put both men into jail overnight. The next morning, a trial of sorts was held and Peter and John were asked a key question. It is recorded in verse 7. (*Read it and share it with the group.*) "By what power, or by what name, have ye done this [healed this man]?"

Verse 10 gives Peter's answer, "Be it known unto you all, and to all the people of Israel, that by the name of Jesus Christ of Nazareth. . . ."—they claimed the power of God through the name of Jesus. Through His name they had authority. In himself Peter was just a man. Not only healing, but verse 12 says something else comes by the power of Jesus' name, and His name only. What is it? Let's read verse 12 out loud together.

Salvation can be explained as being delivered or rescued. As sinners we are in danger of death and hell—in salvation we are delivered from both. We are safe! Only Jesus has the authority to save anyone. No other name under Heaven or on earth, known or given among men, carries with it that power. Religious leaders tell us that salvation can come through other men. This is not true. Only through the name and authority of Jesus can any person be saved.

Live It

One fall day two men were talking. Mr. Johnson shared that he had recently been saved. His friend, Mr. Jones, poked fun and asked, "Oh, yeah, so what has Jesus done for you?" Mr. Johnson repeated as kindly as he knew how. "Why, He saved me!"

"Oh, yeah," teased Mr. Jones, "and just what does that mean?" Without another word, Mr. Johnson leaned over and made a circle of leaves on the ground. He found an earthworm and placed him gently into the center of the circle. Then with a match he set fire to the leaves.

As both men watched, the fire became intense and the heat began to get to the worm. He twisted and turned every possible way, trying to escape his approaching death. Just when it appeared that there was no way out and the worm would be burned in the flames, Mr. Johnson reached into the circle and grabbed him out.

"That's how it was with me," he explained. "When I finally realized that there was no way to escape, Jesus rescued me from sin." How about you? In whose name are you counting on for salvation? The Lord Jesus will rescue you from death. By the authority of His name He wants to do it today.

To the Instructor: Make It Visual

The instructor may desire to display a magazine picture of

a police officer to drive home the opening narrative. It is helpful to have a file of pictures available that you have cut from magazines. When you need one to teach, your time of searching will be greatly reduced if you have a ready file.

Students will enjoy acting out the story of Peter and John and the lame man. Simple robes will serve as costumes. The lame man needs a cup to collect money. Others may be the crowd who react to his healing. This sort of activity takes time, but is very helpful in increasing student involvement and thus deepening insights and memory. Give it a try. Your students will love it. (You may, too!)

SALVATION BY
THE CROSS ALONE

Scripture Text: *"But as many as received him, to them gave he power to become the sons of God, even to them that believe on his name" (John 1:12).*

Lesson Aim: The student will be able to explain that good deeds, love and kindness do not decide if we are headed for Heaven or hell. The difference is if we have received Christ as Savior. The student should evaluate his destination.

    Note: This lesson calls for the use of transparency #4 from Basic Bible Doctrine, the Moody Press series on "Sin and Salvation." However, you can use flannelgraph figures, or simply draw stick figures on a poster or the chalkboard.

Are You Ready?

How did the lame man become well? (Peter, in the name of Jesus, told him to stand and walk.) What kind of power did Peter and John possess? (To rescue from danger, to deliver.) How do you get salvation according to Acts 4:12? (Through the name of Jesus.)

Please study this diagram carefully (#4 from *Basic Bible*

Doctrine, Moody Press series on *Sin and Salvation*). Tell me how these men are the same. (They are dressed alike, both on a path, coming from the same place, both doing good deeds, showing kindness and charity.) How are they different? (They are going different directions and have different destinations.)

See for Yourself

Does the Bible talk about good deeds, kindness and charity? Yes, it does. (*Listen as different students read to you. Hand out before class the following passages to read: Matthew 5:44, Ephesians 4:32, and 1 John 4:11.*) We know it is not wrong to do these activities; in fact, repeatedly there are commands to be involved in them.

Proverbs 16:25 gives an important clue as to what the difference is between these two men. It reads, "There is a way that seemeth right unto a man, but the end thereof are the ways of death." Both men appear to be doing fine. What you can't see is where they came from and where they are headed. (*Add a cross to transparency #4—all from Moody Press Basic Bible Doctrine #1.*)

The man on the top path has come through the cross. He has stopped to realize that he is a sinner and falls short of the glory of God (Rom. 3:23). He has accepted Christ's blood sacrifice to take away his sin. He is a Christian. His sins are forgiven. He knows Christ died for him and has accepted God's payment for his sin. He is now busy doing good works, and showing kindness and love to others because he loves the Lord. John 1:12 is true in his life.

The man on the lower path has not stopped at the cross, so he continues to be guilty before God. He is not forgiven but is condemned before God. He is no better or worse, on the basis of his own life, than the first man. Yet, because he has not come to the cross, he cannot please God (Rom. 8:8). His life appears to be the same. He does good works, is kind and loves those around him. (*Lay #4A transparency over #4; see details above.*)

The first man is forgiven, the second still condemned. The first man is headed for Heaven. John 3:16 and 17 promise him that he will live forever. He has a great reward ahead—not because of what he has done in himself but because he has "come through the cross."

The second man is headed for hell. In spite of all the good things he does, the path appears right but the end of it leads to death! How tragic! John 3:36 says that those who believe not Jesus will not see life and God's anger remains on them.

Live It

What is the real difference between these two men? (*Allow time for participation. This is critical! You will know from this whether the students have understood what you said.*) The difference is in their choice at the cross. One received forgiveness; one is still condemned. He chose not to go through the cross. Which path are you on?

Four young boys decided one day to go exploring in some caves near their home. They had taken a guide along who knew the caves well. One of the explorers really was afraid of getting lost in the caves and not being able to retrace his steps to the outside. All along the wall he used chalk to draw arrows pointing to the entrance.

After spending the morning exploring different tunnels, and taking time for a brief snack, the group began to return to the entrance. The guide led the way with the others following. When they came to the first arrow, the guide went in the opposite direction of the arrow. The fearful boy protested, explaining what he had done with the chalk. The guide assured him that the arrow was wrong. Three boys followed the guide and eventually came to the entrance. The fearful boy followed his arrows and went deeper and deeper into the cave. He was lost. What he did not know was that some other boys had entered the cave and reversed the arrows.

His path seemed right but it headed to destruction. Are you on a path of doing good deeds, hoping it will lead to

Heaven? Determine today whether you have ever been to the cross. You may be forgiven and be sure of your destination.

To the Instructor: Make It Visual

Caution!!! Today's lesson theme is partially symbolic. There has been an effort to explain in concrete, non-symbolic terms the truth of salvation by the cross alone. Children understand whatever they hear literally. If they are taught abstractly, they will interpret that truth literally. They may respond to you by asking if you have ever walked through a giant cross-shaped door. They have taken as a literal door what you meant to describe as a time of decision or consideration of salvation.

You will need the Lord's help to teach them to understand the sweet truths of the Word. They must be taught in a way that they can really perceive. Pray through your presentation to them. Make an effort to think as they do.

THINGS CANNOT SAVE YOU

Scripture Text: *"For by grace are ye saved through faith; and that not of yourselves: it is the gift of God: Not of works, lest any man should boast"* *(Eph. 2:8, 9).*

Lesson Aim: Students should be able to name three of four things that cannot save them. They should be able to quote the opening phrase of Ephesians 2:8.

Are You Ready?

As we display different things that cannot save you from sin, see if you can explain why this is so. Money is necessary for everyday living. People give amounts of their money to churches and charities. Will this take away our sin? (Answer: No, salvation is a free gift.) Cain's sacrifice to God was vegetables and fruit that he had grown. What was wrong with his sacrifice? (It was not a blood sacrifice.) Going to church is a favorite way for lots of religious people to show God they really love Him. Will attendance there save a person? (No, we can learn about God at church, but we don't earn merit by going.) Praying is talking to God. If we talk to Him enough, won't He forgive us? (Praying is not a way to convince God we are good enough for Him. We will never do that—we are sinners.)

Let's study an important verse to see what can save us. It also explains how we are not saved.

See for Yourself

Open your Bible to the book of Ephesians. We will look closely at chapter 2, verses 8 and 9. There are several words that we hear often but don't know what they really mean. You may have already memorized this verse—if not, you should. This is a very key verse in understanding how salvation is and isn't attainable.

Let's look first at the two things that are *not* involved in our being saved. Can you name them? First, salvation is not of ourselves. It has nothing to do with us. It has everything to do with God and what He does. Second, it is not of works. It is not of efforts, deeds, and doings we are involved in. We are even given the reason why works don't count toward salvation. If it were possible for us to work for our salvation, we would boast or get puffed up about our accomplishment.

Read the opening phrase out loud with me. "For by grace are ye saved through faith. . . ." What are the three key words in this statement? Grace, saved, faith. Often these terms are used improperly. Often heard, they may easily be confused. Listen, oh, so carefully to these explanations.

What are we by grace? We are saved. To be saved is to be delivered from hell and death. It is to be rescued. Who can do that for us? Remember that it is not of ourselves, and not by works; God is at work to save us. He alone can guarantee forgiveness of sin and our safe arrival in His Heaven.

So being saved is the result of God's work on our behalf. The key word "grace" explains how He accomplishes it. Grace can be explained, at least in part, as God's free and undeserved goodness. It is free in that it costs us nothing. It cost God His only Son. He pours on us great heaps of goodness, all of which we do not deserve. That is God's grace. It works to save us. Now tell me again, what is grace? (God's free and undeserved goodness.)

Faith is the final key to this great treasure. God's goodness, so undeserved, is nevertheless active in everyone that is saved. When we express or convey to others what God has done in us we are using faith. Faith could be capsulized as a persuasion, a conviction of the truthfulness of God. We realize what is true about God and admit to others that it is indeed true for us.

God saves you and me. He does it by grace, His undeserved goodness. We realize what has taken place and, being convinced of it, tell others. The telling of it, the being convinced of it is faith.

Live It

Money, good deeds, church going and praying cannot save us. Only God's gift can save us! God's gift comes to us through the death of Jesus on the cross. His blood sacrifice allows God's grace to be put into action for us.

A strong but uneducated Chinese boatman poled a flat-bottomed boat up the great Yellow Chinese River. His passenger was a well-dressed and highly educated businessman. The businessman was trying to make the boatman feel stupid. "Do you know geography? Can you read or write? You don't know arithmetic either, do you?"

The boatman was anxiously watching the sky. A severe storm approached. "Sir," he announced, "that storm may tip our boat. You may be rich and educated, but that won't save your life. Can you swim?"

The businessman turned pale, for he could not swim. The storm tipped the boat and he drowned while the boatman swam to safety.

You may be counting on things to save you. Remember, "For by grace are ye saved through faith. . . ."

To the Instructor: Make It Visual

Moody Press overhead series, *Sin and Salvation,* has

excellent visuals for both the opening and final sections of this lesson (transparency #5).

You may find it helpful to hand out slips of paper for students to write down definitions of grace, saved and faith. Continue to display the verse for all to see as you discuss it. Some students will not have a Bible for their personal use. Have your Bible open as you teach. It is a powerful visual way to show that it is an important book. Even though your study is complete, the students need to observe you handling and referring to your Bible.

THE NEW MAN

Scripture Text: *"Therefore if any man be in Christ, he is a new creature: old things are passed away; behold, all things are become new" (2 Cor. 5:17).*

Lesson Aim: The student will be able to recall three new things for every Christian: new Spirit (Holy Spirit), new soul (personality) and new body (at a future time).

Are You Ready?

Have you ever played the game during which one person leaves the room and someone who remains changes something about their clothes? Upon returning, "it" has to determine what change was made. Sometimes it's very difficult to tell. Our study today is similar to this.

During all of the lessons thus far, we have talked together about what sin is, what salvation is and how we can and cannot be saved. Today's lesson will help us to understand more about those who are Christians. We will talk about three very important changes that have happened in them. None of these changes can be seen with your eyes but they are real and noticeable—if you know what to look for. After we learn what they are, you may do a detective job on yourself to see if they have happened to you. Are you ready?

See for Yourself

Our study begins in 2 Corinthians 5:17. The opening few words will tell you what individuals are described here. Who are they? Those who are in Christ. That is another way to say those who are Christians, the ones who are saved. This description fits every man who is in Christ. It could be an indicator, a way for others to know of his faith in Christ.

The verse says he is a new creature. One translation says he is a new creation. In other words, the Christian has been made new by God. Being made new has some exciting changes involved in it.

What has happened to old things? They have gone away. It sounds rather final and deliberate. The old sin, the old guilt, the old destination and the old master are gone! In salvation they become part of the past. They cannot rule the life of this one who is created new.

What takes the place of the old things? New things. God never takes anything away without giving something in its place. The word "new" has the meaning of being fresh, recent, newly made.

Other passages in the Bible will give us help about the three changes for everyone in whom the old has passed away and the new has come. Check 1 Corinthians 2:12 to find the first change.

First, God gives us His Spirit. We call Him the Holy Spirit or the Holy Ghost. He is a real Person, not a pretend idea or someone we make up. He is from God, and is given to us so that we might know the other things given to us from God. In other words, He is our Teacher. So many new things happen to a new Christian that He comes as our personal Instructor. You cannot feel or touch the Holy Spirit. He has no body of His own. He moves into your heart and explains the truth about God. What you couldn't understand in the Bible before now begins to make sense. Why? Are you smarter? No, but you do have a new Teacher. You have a new Spirit.

The second change is explained in 2 Corinthians 3:18. This verse says believers see the Lord Jesus and His Person. Slowly we are changed to look like Him. This is a new soul. It has to do with our personality, habits, attitudes and character. The verse says we are changed from glory to glory. A process takes place. It takes time, but slowly and surely we begin to act, think and be more like the Lord Himself. It doesn't happen all at once. Our old patterns were practiced for a long time and they became habits. So, too, with the new soul. We must allow the Lord to make His changes in us. Slowly, slowly we are changed. God is at work in us to do this. We have a new soul.

The final change we will look at is described in Philippians 3:20, 21. Read it and tell me what you have found. When the Lord returns from Heaven we will have new bodies. What a trade! Our old, sick bodies for new bodies of glory. They will be like His body. The older you get the more this promise will mean to you. The sin of our world causes our right-now bodies to be sick, broken, in need of medicine and rest. Our new bodies will be without all of those defects—they will never get sick or worn out. They won't even get old. This is for all who are in Christ.

Live It

Name them now, the three new things that have come: (1) new Spirit—the Holy Spirit to teach us about God; (2) new soul—a slowly changing personality, habit pattern, attitude always more and more like the Lord Jesus; (3) new body—not yet, but a sure promise when Jesus comes from Heaven.

Detective time. How do you compare? Do you have a new Spirit at work? Or is the Bible confusing, boring to you, making no sense? Maybe you need to be in Christ.

Is your soul becoming new? Or are you more and more unlike the Lord? Are you still caught up in all the old habits and hangups? You won't be all new at once, but there will be a change. How goes it with you?

The new body; well, you'll have to wait on that one. Believe God's promise if you are in Him—it is *sure*.

To the Instructor: Make It Visual

Again, Moody's *Basic Bible Doctrine* has a graphic visual for the lesson. Transparencies #6 and #6A will drive home the three changes.

CONFLICT OF THE OLD AND NEW

Scripture Text: *". . . Walk in the Spirit, and ye shall not fulfil the lust of the flesh" (Gal. 5:16).*

Lesson Aim: The student will explain the conflict of the old man and the new man by giving two representative traits of each. The student should be able to give one of the three possible solutions to the conflict and ask for the Lord's assistance in beginning it right now.

Are You Ready?

Was there a fight at school today? Possibly at lunch, during a recreation time or even during class time today, did a battle of words or fists occur? When a fight breaks out on the playground or lunchroom, what usually happens? A crowd gathers to watch. It's exciting to watch—we want to know who is in the conflict, what the cause was and, most importantly, who will win. Some people say they like to fight; others of us are more than glad to watch (we'd rather not get into it ourselves; we might lose, you know!). People will pay hundreds of dollars in our day to get a ring-side seat at a nationally significant fight. They want to observe the action close up—well, not too close. The other side of the ropes seems to suit them.

We will talk about a fight or conflict today, too. Every believer is involved in this fight, like it or not. We cannot choose to spectate; we are in on this one. We will talk about who is involved, what the results are and, most importantly, how we can help resolve this conflict. If you have your Bible in hand, we are ready to begin.

See for Yourself

Open your Bible to Galatians 5:17 and read out loud what you find recorded there. In order to have a conflict, there must be two opposing people, ideas or thoughts. What are the conflicting items described here? The flesh is one and the Spirit is the other. How do you know they are in conflict? What word (or words) from this verse tells you that? (Answer: "against" [used twice], "contrary to one another.") The word "contrary" includes the concepts of being opposites, to be adverse, to oppose. Thus we have the flesh and the Spirit as enemies. Galatians 5:22 describes more fully the Spirit and His characteristics, while we find more about the flesh recorded in Colossians 3:8, 9. Read them now for yourself.

Make a list of the two opponents. We sometimes call our old nature, the one associated with the flesh, the old man since he has been with every living person since birth. The new nature, which we receive when the Spirit comes to dwell in us, is the new man. (*See lesson on 2 Corinthians 5:17, page 75.*)

Do your lists look like this:

NEW		OLD	
Love	Longsuffering	Anger	Blasphemy
Joy	Gentleness	Wrath	Filthy Com-munication
Peace	Goodness	Malice	Lie
	Faith		

80

From these lists the conflict should be more obvious to you. With both of these natures inside you—the old one from your birth (well practiced and well developed) and the new one (still new but growing)—is there any doubt why it is often such a struggle to live like a new man? The old man did not die or move out when you received Christ. What happened was that the new man moved in, and now there is a battle.

The result of this battle is told at the close of Galatians 5:17. What is it? You cannot do the things that you would or know you should do. Because the old man is present and so evident, we often don't do the right thing. We know what is right, but we automatically do what isn't. The old remainders of sin struggle against God's work of grace so new within us.

As a new believer you have a desire to have the new man in control—to be most evident in your life. How can that happen when the old man is present? Let's look at three keys to the victory for our new man. You will find key number one in Galatians 5:25.

Here we find the instruction to *live in the Spirit*. What is implied is that we allow the Holy Spirit to bend us, to guide us, to influence our choices. He is the HOLY Spirit. He will direct us toward right patterns because He is holy. In prayer, you may ask the Holy Spirit to take control, to move into the drivers' seat of your life. As you do, He will help you walk and carry on everyday living within His control.

Secondly, check Colossians 3:8 and 12 for the next way to let the new man win out. There are two instructions here, one negative and one positive to fill the negative's empty spot. Verse 8 says "take off" all these old qualities. Don't do them any more. Verse 12 continues, "put on therefore." In other words, you do have a choice. It is your will that decides.

Will it be the old or the new? It will take determination, concentration and a strong desire to do right. Determine to do right; begin to do those things that you know are right. You can't be loving someone while you hate them. So begin acting like you love them. There won't be any time left for the old way. Put off the old and put on the new. Sounds like exchanging coats, doesn't it? That is a good illustration of this truth. You don't normally wear two coats. You take one off before you put the new one on.

The third key to victory is tucked away in today's text, Galatians 5:16. One translation puts it this way: "Live by the Spirit and you will not gratify the desire of the sinful nature." We've already looked at the first part. The second part is summarized this way: Don't feed the old man; eventually he becomes weak and loses the upper hand. The old man never gets enough. The more you "feed him" (give in to him), the stronger he gets. Starve him out of control! Focus on developing the new man and his qualities.

Live It

Review the list of qualities describing each man. Which one sounds most like you? Who is in control of your life? Who seems to be winning the conflict? Remember this fight is for life. You can never let down your guard. If you aren't pleased with the present setup, you may make some changes, and the Lord wants to assist you. The promise of Jeremiah 33:3 is true for you. Call upon Him and He will answer.

Which of the three victory keys will you use? Will you live in the Spirit, exercise the "put off, put on" technique and starve the old man? What will you do tonight to begin? Silently pray, talking to the Lord about your decision.

To the Instructor: Make It Visual

The Moody overhead series on *Sin and Salvation* has a good summary of today's presentation. Specifically, number 7 will aid you. This is a good paper-and-pencil lesson. You may want to distribute an outline like the one below for students to work through with the teacher.

CONFLICT

A. _____ vs. _____
  Col. 3:8   Gal. 5:22

B. Result of Conflict   _____
                              Gal. 5:17b

C. Keys to Victory 1. _____
                              Gal. 5:25

          2. _____ , _____
              Col. 3:8, 12

          3. _____
              Gal. 5:16

D. I will _____ with your help, Lord.

What
Is
God Like?

WHAT IS GOD LIKE?

Scripture Text: *"No man hath seen God at any time; the only begotten Son, which is in the bosom of the Father, he hath declared him" (John 1:18).*

Lesson Aim: The student will define attributes as characteristics or traits that set something apart.

Are You Ready?

Describe the things you know to be true about a cat and a dog. How are they different? How do you know if you have a cat and not a dog? (*Allow time for animated discussion and interchange.*) The things you have named about both animals are characteristics. We could also call them attributes. The attributes of a person are some qualities that belong to that particular person.

We will be spending the next nine lessons learning about God. We want to know what He is like. We will come to know how He is unique from all others.

If you didn't know all the attributes of a cat or dog and you wanted to answer my opening question, what would you do? You could find such a creature and then tell me what you observed. Suppose you had never seen a cat and there were none living where you could see them. How would your task be changed?

See for Yourself

As we begin today, we find some startling words. They are in John 1:18. Read the verse and then share the difficulty.

No man has seen God at any time. If no one alive has ever seen God, how can we expect to know Him? (*Encourage interaction on this point. This is a crucial issue. The student needs to formulate an answer that will satisfy.*) If you notice the remainder of the verse, you will discover the answer to this tough question. "The only begotten Son" is brought in here. Who is He? Yes, Jesus Christ is the begotten Son. Where is the Son now according to verse 18?

He is in the bosom of the Father. One translation says, "He is at the Father's side." In other words, they are close to each other. Jesus has been with God and knows what He is like. According to the final few words of our verse, we, too, can know God. Why is that true?

Yes, Jesus has declared Him. We could say that in coming to live among us, Jesus has explained God and made Him known. One father told his children what Jesus did this way: "No one has ever actually seen God, but of course His only Son has, for He is the companion of the Father and has told us all about Him."

Open your Bible to John 14:9 and read aloud what Jesus Himself said to Philip about our knowing God. Begin in verse 8 to get the question. (*Read aloud together.*) If we see and know Jesus, we see and know the Father. Jesus is a visualized explanation of the Father and His attributes.

In coming weeks, as we study the various attributes and their meanings in our lives, we will begin to notice a pattern. Some of these attributes we can possess. Of course, we don't have them to the same extent that God does. Other attributes are special with Him. We can never have them. They are only true of God.

Go through the following list and make up your mind where you think each might belong: love, truth, eternal, holy, infinite, just, unchangeable, sovereign, omniscient.

Like Him	Unique to Him

(When they are done, display the following listing. This exercise will help them to begin thinking about each attribute. First column includes: love, truth, just, holy. Second column includes: eternal, infinite, unchangeable, sovereign, omniscient.)

One final thing we must realize is that there is a danger for those who study these different attributes of God. The danger is that we begin to think of each attribute all by itself. The true picture is that every one of these areas we will study is important to every other one. They each influence all of the others. A favorite word to describe this is "balance." It can be said that all of the traits are balanced to give a whole picture. Imagine a circle of ten children. Each child is holding hands with his neighbors. They form a circle and then take giant steps backwards. As they continue to do so, each pulls and is pulled by his neighbors and others. If someone lets go, the circle is broken and the balance is gone. The shape of the remaining part is quite distorted. So, too, with our study; if we take one attribute and make it bigger, more important than the others, we get a distorted idea about God. Each lesson is important to every other one. All of these attributes are true of God. He has them ALL and in perfect BALANCE.

Live It

What did we say "attribute" means? Someone read John 1:18 for the group. Someone else please explain in your own words what we learn about knowing God from this verse. How can we know God? (By knowing His Son—John 14:8, 9.)

Name one attribute that we can have in common with God. Someone else name another. (*Love, truth, just, holy.*) What qualities does He have all to Himself? (*Eternal, infinite, unchangeable, sovereign, omniscient.*)

Describe why balance is necessary when we talk about what God is like. (Unless we keep them in balance our picture of God is not true—it will be twisted, distorted.)

Do you know God? Do you know His Son Jesus Christ? He wants you to come to know Him today if you don't.

To the Instructor: Make It Visual

Secure a picture of a cat and a dog for your opening time. Make a chart with the categories of "Like Him" and "Unique to Him." You may use either the chalkboard, pocketboard or newsprint with markers. Compare the pictures of the cat and dog, and on the chart list the characteristics that are the same and those that differ under their respective categories.

For the final concept of balance, it would be helpful to use several children to demonstrate balance. Have them join hands and expand the circle until one lets go.

Moody Press has a delightful set of overhead transparencies which demonstrate the balance concept taught here. The series on the attributes of God is essential for this entire unit. Secure a set for your church teaching supplies. They can be used for a multitude of age levels and occasions as you are able.

Sample visual:

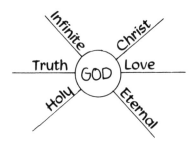

GOD IS LOVE

Scripture Text: *"He that loveth not knoweth not God; for God is love. . . . Herein is love, not that we loved God, but that he loved us, and sent his Son to be the propitiation for our sins"* *(1 John 4:8, 10).*

Lesson Aim: The student will be able to recite the definition for love. The student will be able to determine if love is exercised in a given set of circumstances using the definition. Explanation must accompany all answers.

Are You Ready?

We begin with a short review of the first lesson. Can you recall these answers? What is an attribute? Name some of God's attributes. From John 1:18, please tell who has seen God. Who has not seen God? Why is that so? What does it mean when we say that God's attributes are in perfect balance?

Do you remember the comic strip that was so popular which read "Love is . . ."? It pictured two pudgy little people doing any number of things to and for each other. They weren't really giving a definition of love, but demonstrating love to each other.

Please give me your definitions for love. We will write them down for a better look. (*Allow several to give answers.*) Today we will study what the Bible says about God's love.

See for Yourself

You have given many good definitions. Let me give one and then explain it to you. Love is giving unconditionally for the good of another. So much of what is called love today is not giving but rather taking for oneself. A boy may say he loves a girl but does not respect her person. He really wants to use her, to take her body and use it to please himself. True love involves giving, not taking. If I love you, I will give you what is for your good, not what is for my good. Love is focused on another, not on yourself.

If our definition ended there it would not be complete. Lots of people give to others but not for their best. If you are sick and I give you food, I have given but not, perhaps, for your good. You might really need me to give you a ride to the doctor, to the hospital or to your house. Now you may not like doctors, hospitals or your mom's medicine, but if it will make you better, that is giving for your good.

One final word completes the thought. That word is "unconditionally." It means that the one loving gives *no matter what* the one receiving says, thinks or does. I give to your good. You don't like what I do, but if my giving was truly to your good, I have loved you. And, if you do like this gift, I have loved you. In both situations I have given and in so doing have loved you. It doesn't matter how you felt about what I did. It does not change the love in my action.

Love is giving unconditionally to another's good, whether he likes it or not. Can you repeat this definition?

Open your Bible to 1 John 4:10. Here we find the definition of love in action. Herein is love; or, you could say, here is an example of true love.

Who is the One loving? God is doing the loving. It is specifically stated that we are not the ones who begin this love. Who does God love according to the verse? Us, it says. That "us" referred to Christians living all over Asia Minor in the time of John, but it also means Christians today. How do we know that He loved us, other than that it says so? He sent His

92

Son to be the propitiation for our sins. Is God's sending His Son an act of giving? Why? (*Help students to understand what Christ gave up to come to earth in our behalf.*) The word "sent" means to send on a mission. Jesus Christ did come to earth from the Father to die for the sins of all people of all ages. God's giving was costly. He gave His *only* Son, not one of many.

The word "propitiation" means the satisfaction of someone's rightful anger. God hates our sin. Jesus was given to satisfy the Father's hatred of sin. By His death, Jesus paid for sin.

John 3:16 is a well-known verse in the Bible. Say it out loud with me as we think of our definition of love. God did love; He gave His Son. Was His giving for our good? How do you know? The verse says it is so we won't perish but will have LIFE FOREVER!

Look at John 1:11 and tell how the world responded to God's love. They rejected Him for the most part. Does that change His love? No! Why? Because true love gives unconditionally. Is God's love unconditional? Yes, oh yes!!! It is to all the people of every age. Even YOU.

Live It

We know from John 3:16 and 1 John 4:10 that God is LOVE. Two verses earlier, in 1 John 4:8, we are told that if we do not love each other we do not know God. The reason is that God is love. By knowing Him we should act like Him. He loves and so should we.

Are you a loving person? Do you give to others? Or would you rather take and get for yourself? Maybe you don't know God. Do you give for the good of others? Or do you give for your own good to make yourself look good in the eyes of others? Does the response you receive make a difference in your giving? Will you give if it is well received and hold back if it is not appreciated or acknowledged? If so, you are giving conditionally. Remember, God gave His Son while we were yet sinners (Rom. 5:8).

Andy hated to go anywhere with his mom. You see, her hands were badly marred. They had been horribly burned many years ago. Andy had never even asked how it happened—he was so embarrassed by the fire-melted fingers. Whenever they went shopping, Andy would bring his mom a pair of gloves. That way they would be covered and he would not mind so much being with her.

A lady friend came to visit Andy and his mom one day. During the course of conversation, Andy's mom told the friend about a tragic fire which had nearly taken her son's life in infancy. She had returned from shopping to observe the house in flames. Without a thought for her own welfare, she raced into the house. Covering the baby in her coat, she returned outdoors with her bundle. Her hands were badly burned but the baby had been spared. She was rejoicing to this day in his fine skin and healthy body.

Andy blushed. He had never realized how much his mom loved him. She had given of her very self to keep him alive. Never again did Andy bring mother's gloves. Her hands were proof of her love for him and he was proud.

To the Instructor: Make It Visual

The Moody Press *Basic Bible Doctrine* series has several overhead projection transparencies which very ably visualize this lesson.

Construct a chart similar to this to test the student's learning and skill in applying the definition of love.

Person	Situation	Is this love?	Why?
Teacher	Recess all day long		
Mom	Children may eat all candy in house		
Doctor	Prescribes bad-tasting medicine to cure disease		
Dad	Goes to work every day.		
Parents	Correct you when you are wrong		
Friend	Gives you a present, if you give him one		

A simple heart with the words "God Is Love" will visualize your lesson today.

GOD IS TRUTH

Scripture Text: *"He is the Rock, his work is perfect: for all his ways are judgment: a God of truth and without iniquity, just and right is he" (Deut. 32:4).*

Lesson Aim: The student will be able to recite the definition for truth. He should make specific plans to exercise truth this coming week in his own life.

Are You Ready?

We begin with a review. Since each lesson is important to every other one, we will be doing a lot of review. It gives you an opportunity to show what you know. You must first know God. Then you are ready to grow in your love for Him. Did you know that He *desires* your love? He does!

What is an attribute? Why do we picture the character traits of God in a wheel? What was the definition of love that we studied last lesson? As we review the chart from last week, please tell me which of these pictures true love. Why?

Did someone love you this week? Was their love real and genuine like God's love? God is Love and He takes great pleasure in loving us. Do you love Him? Have you told Him so?

One day as Jesus was talking with His twelve special

followers, He told them three things about Himself. They are written down in John 14:6.

See for Yourself

Open your Bible to John 14:6 and read it to yourself. We will spend today talking about the second attribute Jesus mentions here. What is it? Jesus says that He is the TRUTH. We already know that Jesus shows us what God is like. What does that tell you about God? He is Truth.

Deuteronomy 32:4 gives us two sides of the same idea. It says in part that He is "a God of truth and without iniquity." Usually we define truth as not being a lie. That is an accurate definition, but not a complete one. Webster says truth is "being in agreement with the facts, things, experience; a quality of being certain and reliable." This gives us the positive side of truth. "To tell it like it is," we say in modern language. That's truth—to tell it like it is. To tell it otherwise is to lie.

Three key verses about our God of truth will demonstrate clearly just in what ways He is a God Who tells it like it is. Look up each one and tell how it relates to God's truthfulness.

	GOD OF TRUTH IN:
Deuteronomy 32:4	
Numbers 23:19	
I John 5:20	

The first reference says His Person is Truth. His Being is Truth. He can be no other way, for the very essence of His character is truthfulness. The second reference is found in the account of the prophet Baalam giving his answer to wicked Balak. The answer comes directly from God Himself, through Baalam. We find that what God says is truth. The issue of discussion here is the Word of God. Once He speaks, you can count on it! He will do as He says, for His Word is true. It makes sense that if His Person is true, what He speaks will come from that source and will likewise be true. The final reference talks about God's dealings with us. He deals truthfully. He wants us to know Him as He really is. He has nothing to hide. We are even given the privilege of being in Him. Three times in this one place we are told that He is true. Do we have room to doubt it? He is true, He is true, He is true!

Our definition again relates that He "is in agreement with the facts." Jesus reveals to us that God is true (1) in His Person; (2) in His Word; (3) in His dealings with men.

Live It

Our God is reliable. His Word spoken or written is as good as the accomplished fact. This means two things specifically as it applies to our study of Him. First of all, since God is true, *all of His promises are true.* We can count on them. People make promises and then often fail to carry them out. God is not like that; what He says, He does. For example, God told Abraham that he would be the father of a great nation (Gen. 12:1, 2), that He would give him a land of his own (Gen. 15:7) and that through his family all the world would be blessed (Gen. 12:3). We are told that Abraham believed God. Why could he do that? He could believe because his God is TRUTH.

Secondly, *God's warnings are also true.* He told Noah's generation that judgment would come, but only Noah and his immediate family believed. God kept His promise and all died except Noah and his family. You can count on God's Word whether it be promise or warning. He is a God of truth.

How about you? If you are a child of God, you should be characterized by truth. We are instructed in Ephesians 4:25 to put away lying and to speak every man truth with his neighbor. We are capable of lying. Put it away—don't do it anymore. As believers we should be truthful.

Earlier in that same chapter of Ephesians (4:15), we are

told not only to speak the truth but to do so in love. Using our two definitions, we would say to "give it like it is for the good of another." Our truth telling must be for the good of another. Our purpose should not be to hurt or harm but to help and assist. Some things are better left unsaid. They only hurt and do no good to the one hearing them. Determine right now that this coming week you will be truthful even if it hurts you. Take a moment to pray and share your intention with God. Ask for His help. He wants you to tell the truth.

Consider yourself. Do you tell the truth in love? Is your regular pattern to hurt others with the truth? Remember that God's promises are true; so are His warnings of judgment. Make sure that you are covered by His blood.

To the Instructor: Make It Visual

An open Bible with the words "God Is Truth" written on it will visualize today's lesson. Poster board would be the most desirable for this.

A chart is necessary for your students to respond to the Scripture search in the "See for Yourself" section. It would be best if each student had his own worksheet and pencil. We remember so much longer what we do ourselves. Don't fall into the trap of *telling* everything to your students. Just because you say it does not mean they have heard or understood or internalized your message. Help them to find answers. Your role is that of guide.

GOD IS SOVEREIGN

Scripture Text: *"Come and see the works of God. . . . He ruleth by his power for ever . . ." (Ps. 66:5, 7).*

Lesson Aim: The student will define "sovereign" as supreme ruler. The student should be able to name two things in his world that are under the Lord's control.

Are You Ready?

As the visuals from the first two lessons are shown, let's review what we know already. What does the heart help us to remember (see visual on page 99)? What did we say love means? Does God love us? How do you know?

The book on this poster represents what special Book? What do we learn about God from it? What does truth mean? Tell me two ways that God is true to His Word. (He keeps His promises and His warnings.) Does God expect you and me to speak the truth? Why?

When you see a crown, what kinds of things do you think about? (*Allow time for interaction. Each answer is right because it is personal. Receive them all and slowly begin to focus on the concept of king and ruler.*) We have named a variety of things. Today we will study an attribute of God that is sometimes pictured as a crown. The word is probably new to you, but the idea behind it you may already understand. We say God is SOVEREIGN (pronounced sov-ren).

See for Yourself

The word "sovereign" means to be the supreme ruler of all.

A sovereign is a ruler who makes any and all decisions himself. He has the authority to do what pleases him. He is the chief one, the greatest one. He doesn't have to ask permission for he is the highest in his kingdom. No one can stop him from doing what he chooses.

We don't have any true examples of sovereigns in our everyday situations. Dads are to be the chief in their homes, but the government often tells them what to do. Principals are the authority in the school, but they must answer to the school board. We see a little of the idea of a sovereign from these examples but not in the full way that God is.

Open your Bible to Psalm 66:5-7. While the word "sovereign" does not appear in the Bible, the idea is explained over and over again. These verses are a good example. Verse 7 talks about God's ruling. How long will He rule? Until someone greater comes along? Until He tires? Until Satan overthrows Him? No, He rules forever. No one—you, nor I, nor Satan himself—can overthrow God. What does "rule" mean in this verse? He makes others do as He desires. He has power over them. How does God rule? By His power. In verse 5, His works are described as terrible, not in the sense of cruel or mean, but in the context of awesome. Those who observe God's works are caused to be respectful and reverent, even fearful. His uses His endless power to rule.

Open your Bible to Psalm 93:1 and read to find Who rules. The Lord reigns. What are His clothes? In other words, how would you recognize Him? He wears majesty and strength! What an outfit—He is dressed as a ruler should be. Is the world steady? Why? We see that the world is established— it is firmly fixed and cannot be moved. The sovereign God has the world under control. It does not rule Him but He rules it.

We must keep in mind that God is a Sovereign Who is also loving and truthful. Some rulers allow their power to corrupt them and are cruel. The God of the Bible is not a tyrant or a vicious ruler. He uses His power for the good of others and always in a consistent, truthful way.

Live It

If you knew only of God's limitless power and superiority over men and nothing of His love and truth, you would have reason to fear Him. For the individual who has become a Christian by faith in Christ's death for sinners, this truth about God is very comforting. When hard things come into our lives and we feel out of control, it is good to trust in a sovereign God Who has it all working out for our good. Your God has control of every circumstance and every person who touches your life. If He can turn the heart of the king (Prov. 21:1), He can turn the hearts of those who trouble you. As you pray, leave all of your reasons for worry in His control.

If you do not know this Sovereign as your Ruler, you have reason to fear Him. It is He Who gives you air and health and life. Give yourself to Him today. In so doing you turn His wrath into your protection.

To the Instructor: Make It Visual

A posterboard crown is necessary to visualize the concept of a sovereign. You could intensify the learning by setting up a throne room scene, of sorts, using charts, guards, etc. Dress a leader up as a ruler in a long, royal-looking robe. You will thus focus your students' attention on the function of a sovereign. Be careful to create an awesome setting, not a light, laughable scene, or you may defeat your purpose. Your attitude as the teacher can and will set the response. If you take it seriously, so will the students. Give it a try.

The Moody Press series on *Basic Bible Doctrine #2* has a good set of overhead transparencies for this lesson.

GOD IS HOLY

Scripture Text: *"And one cried unto another, and said, Holy, holy, holy, is the LORD of hosts: the whole earth is full of his glory" (Isa. 6:3).*

Lesson Aim: The student should be able to give "absolutely perfect" as a definition of holy. The student should recall either of two results of our holy God's nature: (1) Heaven is for holy ones; (2) believers should live holy lives.

Are You Ready?

We have spent four lessons talking about God and what He is like. Have you learned something during our time together? Have you changed your idea of Who God is because of something we have studied from the Bible? Please share with the group what you have learned. (*This is a vital time for the instructor. Listen and really hear what your pupils say. Don't squeeze them into repeating your words. If they can retell a truth accurately, they are making significant progress in learning.*)

Today we study an attribute that believers may possess in small measure. God has this quality in full. He not only encourages us to develop it, but we are commanded to strive for it. The name of the attribute is one you have heard often.

We do not talk very often about what it means, so our study should be learning time.

See for Yourself

Almost three thousand years ago, a prophet was confronted with an attribute of God. The circumstances are written down for us in the book of Isaiah. Read with me Isaiah 6:1–4.

What is the attribute described in verse 1? Yes, God is seen as Sovereign on the throne, high and lifted up. Verse 2 describes special angels, seraphim, who are near God. In verse 3 they call out to each other the attribute of God we will study today. What is it? He is holy. What do you think "holy" means? (*Emphasize not only the negative but the positive side of God's holiness.*) Yes, it does mean that He doesn't sin. He is more than that, though. "Holy" means to be absolutely perfect. It has the idea of being physically pure and morally blameless. Never has our God known or committed sin. Always and forever He has done what is pure and right.

Why do you think the angels said "holy" three times? It is most likely for emphasis, so that we don't miss it. They were so aware of His holiness that saying it once or even twice didn't seem to be strong enough.

Read verse 5. How did Isaiah respond as he saw this God Who was so holy? He realized that he was undone or ruined. He continued by admitting that both he and his people, the Jews, were unclean. He realized that he was an evil man. We know from the other chapters of this book that Isaiah was a chosen man of God—he loved God and did His work. Yet, before his God he falls very short.

Sometimes the holiness of God is pictured as a fire or flame. As fire burns it purifies and cleanses (Deut. 4:24). The Old Testament says our God is a consuming fire. The description in Isaiah 6 speaks of a smoke in reference to His holy Person.

Not only is God's Person holy, without sin and absolutely

perfect, but we also see that His actions are holy. Read aloud Exodus 15:11. Moses is directing the children of Israel in a huge choir. They are singing to the Lord, recalling all of His goodness to them. They sing that He is "glorious in holiness, fearful in praises, doing wonders." He is great and magnificent in His absolute perfection. As God had dealt with them and for them He had done so in perfection. How else could He act? His Person is holy and so are His actions.

Live It

That's fine, you may think, for God to be holy. Isaiah may have seen Him but you never have. You aren't a Jew and so their song about His holy ways isn't your song. You are right. What we have learned so far is factual but doesn't directly affect you and your life in the same way it did Isaiah and Moses.

But God's holy Person does mean something to you. Since God is holy, so is the place where He resides. Where is He now? Yes, in Heaven. What is that place like and for whom is it reserved? Heaven is a place for God, His angels and those who are born again (John 3:3). Revelation 21:8 lists a catalog of sins that characterize those who do not enter Heaven. Listen as the list is read. If any of these describe you, you do not have the privilege of entering God's Heaven. In yourself you will never be holy. By receiving Christ's death for your sin, you may become a son of God and so enter. Heaven is a holy place; you will only be holy in Jesus.

Not only is Heaven at stake because of God's holiness, but also your lifestyle is at stake right now. Listen as Peter talks about being holy. (*Read 1 Peter 1:15, 16.*) Peter is talking to Christians. God has called us and He is holy. We are to be holy in the same way in all our manner of behavior. Two reasons are given for us to live holy lives. Do you catch them? Number one: The Holy One has called us. Number two: The Holy One wrote the command long ago when the *law* was first being written. How can we be holy? We must rely on Him

Who is holy. It is not an instant change. Rather, the God Who is holy desires to do a continuing work in us. The goal is before us: "Be ye holy; for I am holy." Begin today with His help!

To the Instructor: Make It Visual

If you desire to have ready-made visual help, refer to the overhead series by Moody Press, *Basic Bible Doctrine #2*. If, on the other hand, you determine to make your own, make use of poster board or overhead markers and transparencies to display the flame symbol and the definition of "holy." Construction paper may also be employed for the flame visual. The final area of application needs to be visual. See illustration below.

GOD IS JUST

Scripture Text: *"He is the Rock, his work is perfect: for all his ways are judgment: a God of truth and without iniquity, just and right is he" (Deut. 32:4).*

Lesson Aim: The student will be able to define "just" as "treats all fairly." The student will determine whether he would receive (1) Heaven or hell; (2) reward or loss of reward; (3) a crown or no crown if God deals justly with him.

Are You Ready?

Define each attribute as it is named and shown. (*Save your visuals each week. They make excellent review tools. Display them, if at all possible, in your teaching area.*) LOVE—giving for the good of another; TRUTH—perfect agreement with facts; SOVEREIGN—supreme ruler of all; HOLY—absolutely perfect.

Mrs. Johnson, the fourth grade school teacher at Washington School, had a very peculiar rule in her classroom. It was her custom to take recess time away from all of the students if any one of them disrupted the room. One particular student caused her difficulty every day. So, day after day, all the children lost their recess because of one noisy individual. What kind of a teacher is Mrs. Johnson? Why?

"There is no dessert tonight for anyone. I'm sorry, but Amy has not eaten all of her dinner," announced Mother to the entire family. "Ah, that's not fair," complained Amy's three brothers and sisters. "We ate ours."

How are these two adults alike? Yes, they are not acting fairly. Today we will study an attribute that means fair.

See for Yourself

God is JUST; that is, He deals with all of us fairly. The Scripture text for today says His work is perfect (holy). He is a God of truth, JUST and right is He. It is interesting how many of His attributes are named here together. Sometimes it is difficult to separate them as they are so closely tied to each other. Yet, here again we see the balance of His Person.

Isaiah 45:21 is a very clear statement on God's justice. Let's read it together. Are there other gods? Are there others who deal justly? No, twice it is stated that God alone possesses this quality. He says of Himself, throughout the book of Isaiah, "I am a just God."

Abraham knew of God's justice and he reminds God of it in Genesis 18:25. Listen as I read to you and pick out Abraham's question. God has said He will destroy the wicked city of Sodom. The question is: Shall not the Judge of the earth do right? Abraham knew God did not deal with righteous men as He did wicked men. Wicked men were to be punished, but in the city there were also righteous men. God's justice would not allow Him to kill both. God delivered the righteous ones in the city and then destroyed it. In so doing, He dealt justly.

Open your Bible to Psalm 18:23–26. Fill in the following chart, using your Bible and pencil.

Those who are:	God deals:
Upright	
	Mercifully
Upright man	
	Pure Froward

The missing words are: according to my cleanness, merciful, upright, pure, froward. Does God deal justly? Why do you think so?

Have you ever seen this symbol? ⚖ Where have you seen it and what does it mean? It is a balance or a device for measuring. When the amount on both sides is equal, the top arm will be parallel to the surface. If one side is heavier than the other, the balance will lean or tip toward that side. We see it often in relation to judges, lawyers and courts. It is a picture of giving punishment equal to an offense. If the punishment is too light, it is not fair. If the punishment is too heavy or harsh, it is not fair. This scale also pictures God's justice. He always measures out the right treatment for us. He is always fair. First John 1:9 says He is faithful and just. He is fair continually, every time He deals with us.

Live It

In closing today, consider three events yet to come in your life. We know that God will deal with us JUSTLY. How will He deal with you regarding the following events yet to come? (1) Heaven and hell. Which will be your future destination? Unless you are God's child, He cannot allow you to enter His Heaven. He must deal fairly. What have you done about your sin? (2) Judgment Seat of Christ (1 Cor. 3:11–15). Will the fire reveal your work as gold, silver and precious stone? Or will your work be burned up and you will be saved but without reward? He is a righteous and just Judge. (3) Crown for service. Revelation 4:10 says that elders had crowns to lay at the Lord's feet. Paul was sure of a crown for himself (2 Tim. 4:8) from the righteous Judge. This crown isn't only for Paul, but for all them who love the Lord's return.

What will the righteous JUDGE give you? Heaven? A reward? A crown?

To the Instructor: Make It Visual

Make your teaching area a colorful, mind-tickling place.

Display your work and that of your pupils. They will learn long after the presentation by the trigger of the visual stimulus. Don't feel you need to be professional or artistic. Some of the most instructive visuals are "homey" and made of stick figures. The students will enjoy your efforts. Enjoy yourself and NEVER teach without making it visual.

Materials are available in the school supply aisle of your drug store, department or stationery store. Use crayons, markers, paper, poster board, anything that is comfortable for you. But *use something!!*

Suggestions:

GOD IS OMNIPRESENT, OMNIPOTENT, OMNISCIENT

Scripture Text: *"Whither shall I go from thy spirit? or whither shall I flee from thy presençe?" (Ps. 139:7).*
"Great is our LORD, and of great power: his understanding is infinite" (Ps. 147:5).

Lesson Aim: The student will be able to give simple definitions for the "omni's." The student will be able to have a time of prayer regarding one of the three and its impact on him.

Are You Ready?

As you begin today, please draw on a sheet of paper a character attribute of God. You may use the pictures we have used together; or, even better, make a picture of your own. Please sign your name near your work so that you may be able to explain to us what you have done.

Today we will study three different attributes. They are only alike because they have the same prefix—"omni." They are each very much a part of our God and make Him what He is. They are important in your life today and tomorrow. These attributes are unique with God. We do not have even a small measure of these; nor can we attain them by any method. Let's learn what they are and give thanks for our great God!

See for Yourself

Open your Bible to Psalm 139:7 and read through verse 10. These verses were written by David. Where does David say he can go to try to escape God's presence? He names Heaven, hell, the morning, the remotest sea, everywhere. His conclusion is that he cannot escape from God. God is everywhere. The word for that attribute is "omnipresent." "Omni" means *all*, so you have a God Who is all-present or everywhere present. The God of David was everywhere at the same time. From the verse we just read you get the idea that God was there before David could get there. Jeremiah 23:23 and 24 say, "Am I a God at hand, saith the LORD, and not a God afar off? Can any hide himself in secret places that I shall not see him? saith the LORD. Do not I fill heaven and earth? saith the LORD."

Now you may wonder how God can do that. You and I can only be in one place at a time, to be sure. We are limited by our bodies. We can be here or there, not here and there, too. God is a spirit (John 4:24). He is a real Person but He does not have a body as you and I do. He is alive, real and free from the limitations of space that we experience. He is omnipresent. Here is one way to picture this truth.

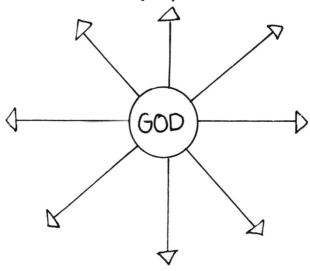

Turn in your Bible to Psalm 147:5. This passage describes the other two omni's. Can you decide what those descriptions are? He is of great power and He is of infinite understanding. Respectively, they are "omnipotent" and "omniscient." What does omni mean? It means "all." "Potent" means "able" or "power," thus "all powerful." You will be familiar with another form of "scient"—science or knowing. God has no limit to His knowledge.

What events in the Bible that you are familiar with show you that God has great limitless power? *(A lively discussion should follow of creation and a multitude of miracles in both the Old and New Testaments.)* Why do you believe that these show God's power and not the wonder of science or a clever trick by man? *(This should cause some creative thinking. Allow time for pupil thought and response. Often teachers program students not to answer by pausing briefly, and then proceeding with their own explanation. Your thoughts are important, but so are those of your students. Encourage them to use their best thinking ability.)*

Genesis 1:1 says, "In the beginning God created [made from nothing] the heaven and the earth." The only Person named as active in the entire creation story is God. He supplies the power for all that is made. The name for Him used in verse 1 means strength, the strong One. The name "Almighty" is used over fifty times in the Bible to describe God. One example is in Exodus 6:3 where God is encouraging His servant Moses. Who wouldn't be encouraged to serve a God of all power!!

Finally, let's consider God's omniscience. What do you think it means to know all? What does God know? He knows everything about the world that we have spent thousands of years trying to learn as men because He created it. There are no secrets from God, nothing He is experimenting to find out about. Not only does He know the universe and all facts, He also knows His creatures. He knows our thoughts, motives and the reasons we have for doing and being. There are no

114

limits to His knowing. We surely do have limits. We forget; we have to go to school; we have to test and explore. Why? Because we desire to know and we don't know things that are necessary to us. Do you agree with the writer of Psalm 147 when he cries out, "Great is our Lord!"?

Live It

Since these traits are true only of God, we should not work to develop them in our lives. They do affect our attitude and manner of living, though, in a definite way.

Consider the following verses, relating them to both God's ability and your need.

	What does it say?	What does it mean?
Matthew 28:20		
I Peter I:5		
Job 23:10		

(This activity may be most easily accomplished as a group project, with different students looking up different verses, while others listen for the answers.)

Matthew 28:20 says, "I am with you alway." God is always with us; we are never absolutely alone. The one who loves God is comforted by this truth, but the one who loves his sin feels uneasy knowing that he cannot hide from God. How do you respond?

First Peter 1:5 says we "are kept by the power of God through faith. . . ." If He is all powerful, there is nothing too difficult for Him. Since we are kept by His power, we need not be concerned about losing our salvation.

Job 23:10 says, "But he knoweth the way that I take." That verse speaks to all of us. If our way is good we will be glad to have Him know. If our way is evil we will be fearful at the thought of having the all-powerful God know it. We will be encouraged to plan wisely because He knows.

Take a minute right now for a word of prayer. Talk to the Lord about getting this settled.

To the Instructor: Make It Visual

The Moody Press overhead transparency in the doctrine series is very suited to this lesson. Here are simple drawings for each of the omni's.

ATTRIBUTE	WHERE IN THE BIBLE	SO WHAT?
	PS. 139 : 7-10	
	PS. 147 : 5	
	PS. 147 : 5	

GOD IS ETERNAL

Scripture Text: *"Before the mountains were brought forth, or ever thou hadst formed the earth and the world, even from everlasting to everlasting, thou art God" (Ps. 90:2).*

Lesson Aim: The student will be able to define "eternal" as not limited by time. The student will be able to show the eternality of God from Psalm 90:2.

Are You Ready?

As you are given definitions of the attributes that we have already studied, please name the attribute.

All-knowing—omniscient

In perfect agreement with facts—truth

Absolutely perfect—holy

Giving for the good of another—love

Treats all fairly—just

Everywhere present—omnipresent

Supreme ruler of all—sovereign

All-powerful—omnipotent.

How many have heard the word "eternal"? What do you think it means? How long do you believe it will last?

Today we study about God's eternal nature. Eternal is a word familiar to most of us. The hard part comes in understanding it. We see time with start-and-stop eyes. We use time cards at work to record when we come in and when we leave each day. We record birth dates and death dates on tombstones. During each school year we think about the next vacation time. We wear watches and have clocks in most rooms and public buildings. Time is important to us.

See for Yourself

Being aware of time is not wrong—God placed us in time. But let's take a different look at it. God's view of time is eternal. He has no birth date or death date. He lives and will live forever. Open your Bible to Psalm 90:2. Read to yourself and count how many time-related words you discover. Please share which words you counted and why. (*Allow one response per child so many may participate.*) Before—indicates a time of beginning; brought forth (born)—time of beginning; hadst formed (made or created)—time of beginning; everlasting—time already gone; everlasting—time yet to come; art—present state of being.

Moses wrote this verse. What was he saying to God? As it appears to man, namely Moses, God Who made the world in time was Himself not limited by time. Moses says God exists right now in three times of history. Can you discover these three times of history in verse 2? The verse shares a time and series of events that are *past* and says God is there. Moses talks about a *future* time and says God is there. And finally, as Moses is writing and talking to God, he speaks as though He were at the *present* time. God is everywhere in time at once. God is not limited by time; He is "eternal."

On a time line, we can indicate the present, the past and the future. Tell me how well you are aware of events in each time. (*Allow several responses and come to a consensus of opinion.*) We see present events pretty clearly. Things from the past are fuzzy. Some memories are very clear; others are forgotten. For example, what did you have for lunch two years ago today? You don't remember? That's normal. You can't know the future for sure. It has a lot of unknowns.

Open your Bible to Psalm 102, beginning at verse 24. How does God see the past, present and future? As we read down through verse 27, we see a man of limited years contrasting himself to a God Whose years go on through all generations, Who will remain the same, Whose years will never end. God sees past, present and future clearly. They all are as an eternal NOW for Him. Second Peter 3:8 says, "be not ignorant of this one thing, that one day is with the Lord as a thousand years. . . ." Our perception of time is so different from His.

Let's read Psalm 90:2 together out loud again.

Live It

As God's time-creatures, we are always in a hurry. We are impatient, anxious, worried and uncertain. We spend so much of the present thinking over the past mistakes and victories and anticipating future troubles that we fail to live in the NOW. God is not restricted to a time-released look at life. He sees all of each life at once. We can relax and trust the future to Him if we are His children and if we have given our past to Him for cleansing.

We see only now, but God sees now, then and when. He sees danger ahead and gives us warning. As we read the Bible and obey it, we will be prepared properly for the future. God sees blessings ahead that can be ours, but we must learn to obey Him now to receive those blessings.

All of the events of Bible history happened before your lifetime. How do you know they are true and accurate? The eternal God was back there and has carefully caused everything you need to know to be written in the Bible.

Have you ever been in a lineup of thick traffic? You sit bumper to bumper for what seems to be forever. If only you could climb a high tree or tower, you could see what the problem was and you would know how to respond. Life is like that. God's perspective includes your future and your past. Rely on Him to direct your way as Psalm 32:8 promises.

119

To the Instructor: Make It Visual

There are several visual aids you could employ today. The students need a sense of time. Have every pupil bring in a clock or watch. Set several timers going in the room. The sound of ticking heightens a sense of time. Use the overheads from the Moody Press series, *Basic Bible Doctrine.*

A simple diagram will illustrate Psalm 90:2.

Use the overhead, poster board, newsprint or chalkboard, but make it visual.

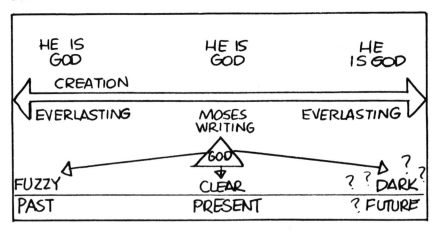

GOD IS INFINITE

Scripture Text: *"Great is the LORD, and greatly to be praised; and his greatness is unsearchable" (Ps. 145:3).*

Lesson Aim: The student will be able to define "infinite." The student will be aware that there is a source of supply for his need (Phil. 4:13).

Are You Ready?

How many attributes of God can you name? Can you also give definitions for them? If you were to draw a diagram of them, what would it look like? Why?

What is a limitation? Yes, it is something that you can't do or that cannot be done. Do you have limitations? It doesn't seem that you have an energy limit, but do you ever go to bed? Why? Your body needs rest and sleep. Why does your mom go to the grocery store every week? She has run out of food. Does your dad ever go to the service station? Yes, he probably needs more gasoline or air or oil. The tank in your car has a limit to the amount that it can hold.

Can you broad jump twelve feet? Why not? There is a limit to your jumping power. Can you throw a softball five miles? Does that sound silly? Well, it is; but the point is clear that we do have limits in many areas of life.

The Bible says our God is without *any* limits. It says He is infinite.

See for Yourself

We must be careful here not to confuse "eternal" with "infinite." What definition did we use for "eternal"? God has no time limits. "Infinite" means no limitations on any attribute. In other words, He possesses time, space, power and knowledge to the very fullest. He never "runs out" or needs to be refilled. He is always full, always giving, always complete.

Open your Bible to Psalm 145, verse 3. This song is David's. Can you almost hear his excitement and reverent worship as he tells God all that He is to David? What word appears repeatedly? Why do you think that is so? The word is "great"; also "greatly" and "greatness." The word as used here means to be large, to be high, noble, of might. The finite man of limitations, David, is trying to explain just how infinite his God is. He says the same word three times in one sentence. He no doubt felt very limited in his ability to even describe this great God of his. The closing word of the verse is "unsearchable." It paints the picture of a scientist in his laboratory trying to number, describe and measure the dimensions of someone who is too big to measure. Have you ever tried to examine someone who is infinite? God is uncountable, unmeasurable in all of His Glory and Person.

The last phrase, "his greatness is unsearchable," could also be rephrased thusly: His mighty acts and dignity can't be figured out. No wonder man with all his limitations can't figure out his God—HE IS INFINITE.

In Job 11:7–9, Zophar speaks to troubled Job and relates God's infinity. He suggests the dimensions of the earth and sea to measure God, but admits they are not sufficient. Paul uses different measuring tools in Romans 11:33, but comes to the same conclusion; namely, ". . . how unsearchable are his judgments and his ways past finding out!"

Live It

What does it mean to you and me that God cannot be

measured? Two different yet important thoughts come to mind. First, as we read Psalm 145 we get a clearer picture of our God and His greatness. We begin to realize just how limited we are. As our thoughts about our abilities become truer to life, God seems even greater. Often we get things out of their true proportions. The tendency is to make ourselves bigger than God and to make Him smaller. That is wrong and harmful to a proper view of life. Do you feel big today? It's not wrong to like yourself, for God made you and He only makes good things. Yet you are still finite—you are human. He is GOD!!

Secondly, God's infinite Person is also loving. He enjoys giving for your good from His supply of endless resources. You never need to fear that He will run out of what you need. Psalm 145:15 and 16 demonstrate this idea. Can you see it and explain it to the group? What does God give to finite men? Verse 15 says He gives food at the proper time. Verse 16 says He satisfies every desire of all the living! Wow! What do you desire? God is able to fill you full.

The New Testament says the same thing this way. "But my God shall supply [cram you completely full] ALL your need [lack or necessity] according to his riches in glory . . ." (Phil. 4:19). How can He do it? He is the infinite God; He has an endless supply. Note that He gives to your necessity, not to your selfish wishes. What do you need today? Salvation? Love? Friends? Food? Warm clothes? Ask God for them. He wants to fill your need!

To the Instructor: Make It Visual

The overhead *Doctrinal Series* from Moody Press will assist you in this lesson if you desire ready-made materials. You will be able to use all of the overheads from earlier lessons to review in the ARE YOU READY? section.

You will find it helpful to have supplemental verses written on overheads or newsprint. It will save time to have this done before class and it will add more weight to an already established point. Students can then follow along without distraction.

A diagram to distinguish "eternal" and "infinite" is a MUST! A possible symbol for infinite can be borrowed from mathematics— ∞. It is limited in its visual impact, but may be helpful for your group.

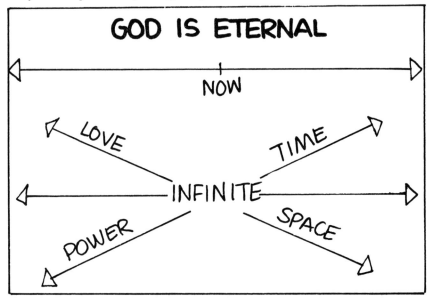

GOD IS ETERNAL

NOW

LOVE   TIME

INFINITE

POWER   SPACE

GOD IS IMMUTABLE

Scripture Text: *"For I am the LORD, I change not; therefore ye sons of Jacob are not consumed" (Mal. 3:6).*

Lesson Aim: The student will be able to define "immutable" as unchangeable.

Are You Ready?

Please take some time today to match each of the following verses with the attribute of God it describes.

Isaiah 6:3	Psalm 66:5, 7
Psalm 145:3	Psalm 90:2
Psalm 139:7	
Deuteronomy 32:4	Psalm 147:5
1 John 4:8, 10	Deuteronomy 32:4

Love, truth, holy, just, sovereign, eternal, omnipresent, omniscient, omnipotent, infinite. (See visual section for answers.)

Have you ever changed your mind? First you wanted a certain kind of ice cream, but the more you thought about it, another kind seemed better.

On the playground you can hear the same boy or girl make these comments just minutes apart: "Jim, you're my best friend." "Oh, yuck, I don't want to be your friend ever again."

125

Why does that happen? Maybe there was a fight or mis-understanding but, regardless, there was a change of mind.

You know the story of Dr. Jekyll and Mr. Hyde. The same man possessed two personalities so different that it appeared they were two separate individuals. But in reality there is one person with two ways of behaving. Today we study about God's stable character. He is unchanging.

See for Yourself

We have already studied ten different character traits of God. We have not learned all there is to know, for He is unsearchable; but hopefully you know more now than when we began. The character quality of today's study touches every other one. The official name is "immutable." That sounds awesome, but actually it means that God doesn't change. He is always the same.

Open your Bible to the book right before Matthew—Malachi. Malachi was a special spokesman for God to His people. Chapter 3 and verse 6 contains the thought we want to explore. Read it to yourself, noting Who is speaking, what He says and the result of what He says. If you decided that the Lord was speaking, you are right. If you said He changes not, you are right again. And if you said the descendants or rela-tives of Jacob are not consumed or destroyed, you are on target!

If our God did change His attitude toward sin and righteousness, we would be utterly confused as to what to believe. He does not change. He has always hated sin and loved righteousness. He always will. If our God changed His character, we would be very unsure of how to approach Him. He is always love. He is always just! He will always be infinite, eternal, truthful, and so on. We may always come confidently to Him, knowing Who He is and how He acts.

Psalm 102:27 adds this thought, "But thou art the same, and thy years shall have no end." Here we see immutability and eternality tied closely together.

Live It

The illustration on the first page of this lesson is of a plumb line. It is a tool used by builders and surveyors. It also is a good way to picture God's immutability. A plumb line consists of a heavy weight attached to a free-moving line. When the plumb is tied on one end, the string will automatically hang straight up and down. Builders use it to make walls straight, to hang doors, to lay foundations. It always hangs straight. There is never a time that it does anything else. God is always the same. How about you? If you are truthful, you will admit that you are not always the same. As a Christian, you should be more and more like the Lord with His help. If you find yourself crooked, ask for His forgiveness.

God does not change. If you are a sinner, He hates your sin. Confess it. If you are His child, don't try to change His mind by praying silly prayers. He will give you what is for your good, not just what you want.

James 1:7 is a great comfort to Christians. God always gives *good* gifts. He will never change or turn from doing what is for our growth.

To the Instructor: Make It Visual

Borrow a plumb line to demonstrate its function to the class. You can make a plumb line with a heavy rock or weight and a string.

Do have ready for distribution the review outlined in the opening. It is important for these character traits to be linked with Scripture texts. They are found in the Bible, and you need to teach your students by challenging them to look them up.

First column answers: holy, infinite, omnipresent, just or truth, love. Second column: sovereign, eternal, omnipotent and omniscient, truth or just.

Transparency #12 in the Moody Press *Basic Bible Doctrine #2* series (The Attributes of God) is excellent for this lesson.

Seasonal
Specials

KNOW THE FUTURE

(Halloween)

Scripture Text: *"I will lift up mine eyes unto the hills, from whence cometh my help. My help cometh from the LORD, which made heaven and earth" (Ps. 121:1, 2).*

Lesson Aim: The student will be able to distinguish between getting knowledge of the future by methods approved by God and by those we are to avoid.

Are You Ready?

This is the season for dressing up, spook houses, orange and black Halloween colors, cider, donuts, hayrides, burning leaves, apples and apple pies. Many of you will trick-or-treat friends and neighbors. Others of you will want to but will decide you are finally too big (for dressing up; certainly not too big for candy!). There is an air of fun and excitement.

While dressing up and having fun are not wrong, there are some real dangers for you during this holiday. We will talk about one tonight. It is important for you to realize how serious this is, although many of your friends may think it is a joke or a funny activity. It is serious, and the Bible has specific instructions for you so you don't get into danger.

We will talk about telling the future. There are right ways and wrong ways to know your future. We will not only discuss these different ways, but why they are safe or unsafe. Put on your ears. . . .

See for Yourself

Open your Bible to Deuteronomy 18:9–14. As you find the place, let me tell you who was talking here and what in general was being said. Moses, the great leader of God's special people, was giving directions for their move to a new land. These people had lived for 400 years in Egypt. God was giving them a new land. The people who lived in the new land were godless. They did not love or worship the true God, and they were involved in many practices that God knew would harm His people, so He warned them.

Read verse 9 to discover who was giving this new land to the Israelites. It says, ". . . the LORD thy God giveth thee. . . ."

Examine verses 10 to 12 and list what practices these people did that God detested. He strongly, intensely hated many of their ways. Your list should include the following:

(Explanations from NIV)

Make son/daughter pass through fire	(sacrifice child on fire)
Use divination	(sorcery)
Observe times	(interpret omens)
Enchanter	(engages in witchcraft)
Witch	
Charmer	(casts spells)
Consulter with familiar spirits	(mediums)
Wizard	(spiritist)
Necromancer	(consults with the dead)

Verse 12 tells you how God feels about these practices and what He did about the ones who practiced them. Tell what both are. They are abominable—*He hates them!* God drove out these people with their sinful ways. The people of God were not to take part in these activities—not even in a joking or light way. God's instruction is given in verse 13. What were they to do? They were to be upright and sincere with the Lord. He implies that to be involved in this list of activities is to be in *sin* and to be without sincerity before God. One translation puts it this way: "You must be blameless before the Lord your God." No room for experimenting there.

Verse 15 tells how the Israelites were to know the future. God does not want them to be ignorant. He is interested in the way they determine the future. Explain how they were to know future events. The Lord was going to send a prophet to tell them all they needed to know.

Live It

You may know someone who practices sorcery or interprets omens. Today, more people than ever are openly involved in the spirit world. The methods of telling the future given in Deuteronomy are very up-to-date. We are bombarded with people who claim these powers. From what we studied in Deuteronomy, what do you believe God intends for us to do about them? Should we learn their ways? Why or why not? Should you spectate and enjoy while someone else participates or practices these activities? Why?

God never changes! The God Who hated these ways in Old Testament times still hates them today. We don't have prophets today to tell us what we want to know about the future. Where is our source of help? Psalm 121 says the hills, where the Lord is. Worshipers sang this song as they climbed up the hill to Jerusalem, for hills were a symbol of God's strength. Much of the future of the world is recorded in the prophetic books of the Bible. Study the Bible if you wish to know about the future, your life and your eternal home. Everything you need to know is recorded there.

Where do you go for help? To the Lord or to the fortune-tellers? "I will lift up mine eyes unto the hills, from whence cometh my help. My help cometh from the LORD, which made heaven and earth" (Ps. 121:1, 2).

To the Instructor: Make It Visual

If tonight is a special night, any decorations you have in your room should lend themselves to the theme. A chart is necessary to list wrong ways to know the future. See the idea below:

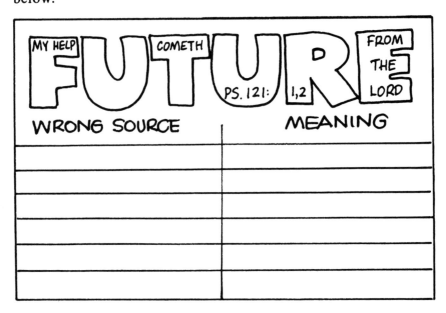

ONE SAYS THANKS
(Thanksgiving)

Scripture Text: *"It is a good thing to give thanks unto the LORD, and to sing praises unto thy name, O most High" (Ps. 92:1).*

Lesson Aim: The student will determine to share specific thanks with one individual during the coming week.

Are You Ready?

Are there times when you don't feel thankful? Something has been given to you and you feel like the other individual owed it to you. You don't say thank you or, if you do, you don't really feel thankful.

A psalm we will talk about today tells us that it is a good thing to give thanks to the Lord. There are many reasons why we ought to give thanks and we will talk about them today.

The apostle Paul told Timothy that there would come a time when unthankful people would be in the majority. Could we have arrived already?

Are you a thankful person? Should you be? Does God expect you to express thanks? Isn't it enough to be inwardly grateful? Put your thinker in gear and let's begin.

See for Yourself

Our study today is in Luke, chapter 17. We will be reading

and talking about verses 11 through 19. Read the entire section aloud with me. Ready? Read.

Who is the central Person here? Jesus is the focal individual in this account. Where was He going? What way did He go there? He was on His way to Jerusalem. Evidently He was on the border of the two provinces of Galilee and Samaria. Samaria was considered foreign territory and the Samaritan people were hated by the Jews as outcasts. Evidently (v. 12) Jesus was about to get some food or drink and rest before He continued on, as we have recorded His entry into a village.

Who did He meet? Why did they stay afar off (v. 12)? Ten men were together in a group. We get the impression that they were looking for Jesus. They stood at a distance because of a disease that they had—leprosy. Those who had leprosy were not to have close contact with others so it would not spread.

How do you know they were interested in getting Jesus' help (v. 13)? They raised their voices, calling out to Him. They used two titles of address—Jesus and Master.

What was their request (v. 13)? Have mercy or pity on us. They did not ask specifically for healing. The mercy of this Jesus was sufficient for them.

Jesus' instruction to them will seem unusual, but the law required that a priest verify healing before a healed individual could return to normal living. He told all ten to go. They were not yet healed, we know from verse 14, but as they went they were made clean. As they obeyed and went, healing was theirs!

One of them realized that he was well . . . stopped and returned to Jesus. The others must have noticed what he did—he was going in the opposite direction. They chose to go on; he chose to return.

Describe his time with Jesus as seen in verses 15 and 16. (*Allow time for several to add information as you reconstruct this thanksgiving service.*) His voice was loud—he wasn't ashamed. He glorified and gave credit to God for what had been accomplished in his life. He fell down on his face at Jesus' feet. That's a humble man for you. He put himself down; his face was lowered; he was at Jesus' feet. Not only did he glorify God, but he gave thanks to Jesus.

What was his nationality? Verse 16 says he was a Samaritan. From all the details in the story it is likely that the others were Jewish men. This man was really a religious foreigner; yet, of all of them, he had returned to say thanks!

All ten were healed. Being thankful was not a condition of cleansing. Jesus asked him where the others were, but no reply is recorded. They were all well—nine because of Jesus' compassion and one because of his faith. He was to go his way. Jesus had declared him whole. It is interesting that Jesus expected all of the men to give thanks.

Many ask for mercy from God, but few return to worship Him and give glory to God and thanks to His Son, Jesus. How about you?

Live It

The song recorded in Psalm 92:1 says it is a good thing to give thanks unto the Lord. The Samaritan man understood what this meant. Not only is it pleasing to God to give thanks, but it is also good for us.

God's blessings are on your life. He gives you life, air, food, family, work, a place to live. Are you like the thankless Jews who went on their way or the Samaritan who returned to say thanks?

Determine right now one person that you will share a "thank you" with this week. Who is the person? When will you speak to them? Will you determine before God to do it this week?

Are you a thankful person? You should be. Does God expect you to give thanks? "Where are the nine?" Jesus asked. Yes, we are to give thanks.

To the Instructor: Make It Visual

A map will be necessary to point out Galilee and Samaria and the city of Jerusalem. Your church may already have a teaching picture available of this narrative; use it. You may wish to dramatize the lesson with the use of stick figures.

TO TELL THE TRUTH
(Washington's Birthday)

Scripture Text: *"Jesus saith unto him, I am the way, the truth, and the life: no man cometh unto the Father, but by me" (John 14:6).*

Lesson Aim: The student will be able to list the two steps in learning to be truthful.

Are You Ready?

"My name is Adeline Moore." "My name is Adeline Moore." "*My* name is Adeline Moore." And so begins another episode of the popular television game show, "To Tell the Truth." Three individuals all claim to be the same individual. A panel of "experts" try to determine who they really are, for only one is telling the truth.

The first president of our country was known to be a man of great truthfulness. The familiar account of his boyhood expedition of cutting down a cherry tree is immortalized. George Washington was a truthful boy who grew to be a truthful, trustworthy young man.

We have a God of truth. Today our focus is not on famous people who were truthful or even on the God of truth. You and I are in focus today. Are we truthful even when it is to our advantage to tell only part of the truth? Why tell the truth? What should you do if your practice is to lie or tell half the truth?

See for Yourself

We will draw a contrast between truth and lying. We will be using a number of different verses to get the overall picture. (*You may want to assign texts to different ones to save time in looking each up as a group. Do read all the verses aloud.*)

First, examine the Person Who is the source of truth and the one who is the source of lying. You will find Psalm 31:5 and John 8:44 to be of assistance. Who is the source of truth? David says that the Lord God is Truth. The essence of His Person is Truth. Every time He speaks or acts or deals with us it is in truth. John 8:44 reveals the devil or Satan as the original liar. There is no truth in him, so how could he speak the truth? He is the father of all lies. The old saying, "Like father, like son," holds here, too. If you are a child of God, you should speak the truth. If you are a child of the devil, you will be a liar just like him.

What we speak, truth or lie, affects us. Check Psalm 91:4 and Proverbs 6:16 to determine the effect of each. We find that God's truth is a shield and buckler. Both are defensive weapons. One protects your person and one protects a larger group or area. In the discussion of spiritual armor in Ephesians, truth is mentioned again as vital protection. Of the seven listed items which activate God's anger in Proverbs, two relate to lying—a lying tongue and a false witness that speaketh lies. God loves sinners but hates their lying!

There is a vivid contrast to the continuing quality of truth and non-truth. See for yourself the difference in Proverbs 12:19. Truth is established forever. That's a long time! I'd like my words to last that long. Lies remain only for a moment and are quickly gone. How long will your words last? Forever or for a moment?

The last consideration today is the result of telling the truth or being a continual liar. Both are established, learned patterns and both will receive specific results. See for yourself: look at John 8:32 and Revelation 21:8. The truth has the capacity and effect of making you free. God is truth and by knowing Him you will be free to live as you ought to. Freedom does not come from doing whatever you want. Rather, as you know and live in truth you will be truly free. The Revelation passage is a frightening yet truthful record of liars' destination. They will have their part in the lake which burneth with fire and brimstone. This is a second and final death. Since God is truth, He cannot allow those who lie to live with Him. They are sentenced to a future of separation from the God of truth in the fire of hell with the father of lies.

Live It

We have discussed the source of truth—God; the source of lies—Satan. Truth is a protection; lying brings God's anger. Truth lasts forever and lies are but for a moment. The final result of truth is freedom. Those who are liars have a place reserved in a fiery judgment forever!

How about you? What is your attitude regarding truth and lying? The passages we have looked at are accurate and will surely come to pass. Don't believe Satan's lie that you can avoid the truth and still be free, without danger. It just isn't so!

If you are a liar, confess your sin to God. Tell Him you are sorry. Ask for His forgiveness. Begin to practice Psalm 119:30 and Proverbs 23:23. Step one: Choose the way of truth. Make up your mind and don't allow anyone to move you. Seek God's help! Step two: Buy the truth and sell it not. Treat truth like valuable gold or jewels. Always be gathering truth. Treat truth with respect and care.

There was once a young boy who was a chronic liar. His dad was concerned about this and determined to help the boy realize the seriousness of his offenses. Every time the father caught the boy in a lie he made him pound a nail into the barn door. Each time he told the truth, he was permitted to remove a nail.

At first, the barn door was receiving nail after nail. When it was nearly full, the boy realized the seriousness of his problem. As he prayed and asked for God's forgiveness, he determined to tell the truth.

Nearly a month later he removed the last nail. With the Lord's help he had established a good habit—telling the truth. When he took his dad to see the door, the young boy began to cry. He had seen for the first time the ugly holes which the nails had left. He had been forgiven but some of the damage of his lying still remained.

If you lie, you too are doing permanent damage to yourself and others. You may be forgiven but you may live with the scars. Determine today to tell the truth!

To the Instructor: Make It Visual

A picture of George Washington is necessary for the opening. You will need to prepare a chart to summarize the study search. Fill it in as you go along. If you bring a filled-in chart, students may feel they are playing a guessing game. They need to sense that their ability to find answers in the Bible is worthwhile. Use their responses. See the diagram on the following page.

For the final section it would be appropriate to have a piece of wood and several nails. As you relate the story, demonstrate the process the little boy experienced. This will be much more vivid for pupils than merely telling the story. You may allow a student to help.

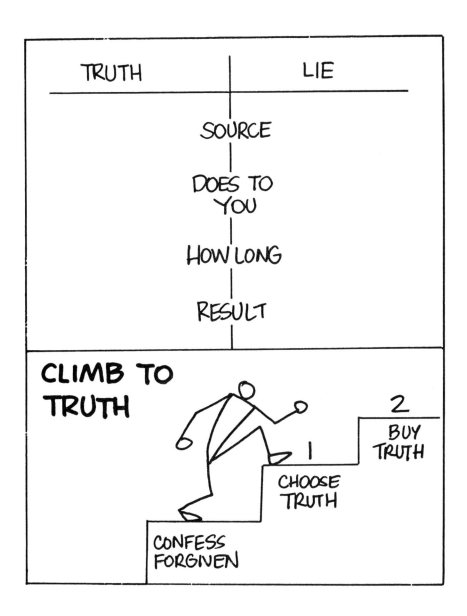

TRUTH	LIE
	SOURCE
	DOES TO YOU
	HOW LONG
	RESULT

CLIMB TO TRUTH

CONFESS FORGIVEN

1 CHOOSE TRUTH

2 BUY TRUTH

I CAN LIVE FOR GOD THIS SUMMER

Scripture Text: *"I sought the LORD, and he heard me, and delivered me from all my fears" (Ps. 34:4).*

Lesson Aim: The student will decide on one course of action that will cause his summer to be positive spiritually.

Are You Ready?

Summer is coming! Yeah! School will soon be closed for summer vacation. Mom and dad will have some ideas about your summer. You, too, will make plans for fun times and things to do. Some young people take a vacation from the Lord in the summer. They don't actually plan to; it just happens that way.

Summer vacation is no reason to forget all the spiritual progress you have made this year. Today's lesson is entitled, "I Can Live for God This Summer." Is that how you feel? Philippians 4:13 is a good promise: "I can do all things through Christ which strengtheneth me." You can make this summer count for God. Notice the positive attitude of Paul—I *can*. He doesn't say I might, I think I could or maybe I should try. You, too, *can* do all things through Christ.

See for Yourself

Step one: a strong desire to live for God (Phil. 4:13). We

have already shared this idea together. The point is, do you agree? Yes, Paul wants to do all things through Christ. How about you?

Step two: make good plans. Many people with good intentions never get any further. Why? They make no plans, set no goals, have no target. Don't allow your summer to pass away while you rely on good intentions. Four areas are discussed below. Each passage of the Bible does not talk specifically about the activity named, but gives principles which should help you. Your task is to make an application (i.e., take the principle and give a suggestion for the activity).

Activity	Bible Passage	Principle	Suggestion
Reading	Philippians 4:8		
Music	Psalm 19:14		
Television	Psalm 101:3		
Friends	Proverbs 13:20		

(Allow plenty of time for work on this activity. You may divide the group and assign passages for time's sake. Make sure you share with the group each verse so students benefit from each other's work.)

Here are some possible answers to your search:

Philippians 4:8—be selective about what you read. Read literature that is true, honest, just, pure, lovely and of good report. Suggestions: Visit the church library once each month. Visit the public library and read books on topics that match the principle. Read your Sunday School paper each week. Read the Bible at least 3 days each week.

Psalm 19:14—words and thoughts must be acceptable to God. Suggestions: Carefully select music that directs your thoughts to God. Exclude music that has suggestive lyrics and a worldly beat and rhythm. Experiment with a new instrument. Learn a new chorus or hymn.

145

Psalm 101:3—set no wicked thing before you. Suggestions: Learn to change the channel on your television when an indecent show comes on. Learn to turn the TV off and find other activities. Don't watch on TV what you won't go to see at a movie house. Enjoy good programs. You are in control, not the TV—act like it.

Proverbs 13:20—develop friendships with wise people. Avoid fools! Suggestions: Take care in picking friends. Work at having a friendship with someone older than you. Develop friendships with Christians via youth and church activities. Join the church softball league, and attend church activities

Live It

You may have super intentions and make great plans, but without the Lord's help you can do nothing. Psalm 34:4 reminds us that the one who seeks the Lord, looking for help, is heard. God promises to deliver us from fear.

Look over your chart. Which area will you determine to work on especially? Circle that area. Which specific suggestion will you ask the Lord to help you do? Place a check by it. Take a moment for prayer and share with the Lord what you have decided.

To the Instructor: Make It Visual

A chart of information and space to work, as outlined in See for Yourself, will be needed for each pupil. Have pencils or pens ready, too. If your group is too young to do this alone, walk them through each verse, filling in the blocks as you go. The concepts are not too difficult, but the student may be lacking in writing and abstract thinking ability.

You may want to display a variety of pictures of summer activities around the room to get the students thinking. You could engage them in a limited discussion of "what will you do this summer?"

HIS NAME IS WONDERFUL
(Christmas)

Scripture Text: *"For unto us a child is born, unto us a son is given: and the government shall be upon his shoulder: and his name shall be called Wonderful . . ." (Isa. 9:6).*

Lesson Aim: The student shall be able to identify the child of Isaiah 9:6 as Jesus. The student shall be able to define "wonderful" as singular; there is none like Him.

Are You Ready?

Sally comes skipping and bounding into class. "I have a baby brother, I have a baby brother," she half sings, half shouts. Sally continues to share the exciting news of her new brother and the events that led to his birth. One of the first questions that Sally's friend Diane asks is the baby's name. Sally tells the baby's name and how the decision had been reached. The baby's name is very important. Each member of the family usually has a special someone that they want to name the baby after. There is significance in a name.

Webster says a name is "a word or phrase by which a person is known, called, or spoken to or of. A word or words expressing some quality considered characteristic or descriptive. . . ." In a certain sense you become your name.

Today we begin to study the names of a baby Who was yet

to be born. The names will give us an understanding of what He would be like.

See for Yourself

Open your Bible to Isaiah 9:6 and read with me. According to this verse, to whom was a child to be born? The verse says "us." It refers to the Jewish people. Is this child to be a boy or a girl? How do you know? The next phrase tells us, ". . . unto us a son is given."

The child spoken of here was born over 700 years later. These people waited a *long* time for this unique One. They knew much about Him from His names, but not until the time of Caesar Augustus did they know Him. He was born in a feed bin for animals. His name was Jesus.

Today we will take a special look at the One called Wonderful. That name is singular; there is none like Him. He is unique, one of a kind. This One is Jesus and His name is Wonderful.

Read Psalm 119:129 and tell one specific thing that is wonderful about Him. His testimonies (laws) are one of a kind. They are special and the writer is committed to keeping them. His laws are for our good and are fair, true and right.

We have already learned that His *name* is Wonderful from Isaiah 9:6. Have you ever looked in the phone book under Smith, Jones or Johnson? Those names surely aren't one of a kind or singular. The list seems to be endless.

Finally, take a look at Isaiah 25:1. What else is wonderful about Him? Not only are His laws and His name wonderful, His works are wonderful. "I will praise thy name; for thou hast done wonderful things. . . ." Yes, this Jesus is wonderful in all His ways. The Gospels are filled with account after account of His special and unique ways.

John 4 records a special encounter with a woman who didn't know Jesus. After a short exchange of words she says in verse 19, "I can see that you are a prophet." She realizes there is something different about this man. This woman was looking for the Child to be born, the special Son to be given.

She says she knows Messiah is coming and He ". . . will tell us all things" (v. 25). Jesus openly tells her that He is the One she is looking for.

Was the woman convinced? It certainly seems so. At first she leaves in a rush to return to the city. There she tells the men about the uniqueness of this one. She is convinced that this is the Christ (v. 29). Her testimony was so strong that others believed because of it (v. 39).

Live It

Do you believe that Jesus is wonderful? Are you sure that He is singular—there is none other like Him? Have you received His work for you on the cross? If not, do so now.

Some people involved in oriental religions have a "god shelf" in each house. Jesus is not just another god to add to your list or collection. He is wonderful—there is none other like Him. He *alone* wants to be your Savior and Lord.

To the Instructor: Make It Visual

Child Evangelism Fellowship has a very useful teaching flashcard visual entitled, *My Wonderful Lord.* It would be a ready-made visual for this lesson and entire series. Included are an illustrated introductory story and visualized Bible story for each lesson. This lesson is intended to be supplemental.

It would be appropriate to display during this entire series a large mural of the Christmas nativity in silhouette. Each week add the name for Jesus that is being studied.

HIS NAME IS COUNSELOR

(Christmas)

Scripture Text: *"For unto us a child is born, unto us a son is given: and the government shall be upon his shoulder: and his name shall be called Wonderful, Counsellor . . ." (Isa. 9:6).*

Lesson Aim: The student will be able to define counselor as one who listens, understands and advises. The student will choose to follow the Lord's advice or to go his own way.

Are You Ready?

Have you ever felt that no one wants to listen to you? You begin to tell a friend at school something exciting that happened to you over the weekend and he is talking to you about his weekend. Both of you talk and neither one listens. How do you feel when that happens? Angry? Frustrated? Hurt?

Listening is important. Some people are especially good listeners. They hear not only our words but how we feel about the things we say. They seem to understand, to feel as we do. Somehow a person like that is a real treasure.

Today we discuss another name of the promised Son to be born. How many recall the name we studied last time? What was it? What does it mean? His name is Wonderful. He is unique, singular; there is none like Him.

See for Yourself

Open your Bible and read aloud Isaiah 9:6. What name there means one who listens and understands what you feel? If you selected "Counselor," you are correct.

Have you ever had a counselor? Where? (*Allow opportunity for discussion.*) You have a school counselor. You may have been to camp and had a cabin counselor. What are the duties of the counselors that you have known? (*There will no doubt be a great variety of answers given. They are all acceptable since they are true to the student's circumstance.*) What do you believe to be the most important thing your counselor does?

A counselor is an individual who is wiser than we are. He is able to listen and understand us, yet his most important role is in offering advice. Knowing us and our circumstances, he can suggest the best plan of action either in school or at camp.

The Old Testament tells us of two young men who needed counsel. They were rulers and needed older, wiser advice. Read 1 Chronicles 27:32 and 2 Chronicles 22:2, 3. Name the man, name the counselor and tell what kind of counsel they gave.

David	Jonathan	wise man—wise counsel
Ahaziah	Mother Athaliah	wicked counsel

You know David well enough to evaluate him. Did David follow the counsel he was given? What was the result? Yes, he did follow. His was a good time for Israel. Read 2 Chronicles 22:4 and answer the same questions about Ahaziah. Yes, he, too, followed the counsel. He did evil and ended in destruction. What was the difference between these men? David had a godly counselor; Ahaziah had a poor counselor. What does this mean to you?

You must take extreme care to select a godly counselor. Isaiah 9:6 tells us about a Counselor. Who is He? The Lord

Jesus born in Bethlehem was the Counselor promised to the Jews. There are many occasions recorded in the Bible when people went to Jesus to ask His advice.

Live It

Nicodemus came to ask the Counselor questions about being born again (John 3). Did Jesus answer his questions? Yes. Did Nicodemus follow what he was told? Look at John 19:38, 39, 40. This does not specifically answer that question, but you do find Nicodemus involved in burying Jesus. Had he not believed, it is doubtful that he would have been involved in this process. It seems fair to say that Nicodemus did believe Jesus and followed His counsel.

Jesus is the best Counselor you can have. He is true. Most important, He has been in Heaven and knows God intimately. He desires that you believe His work on the cross was for your sin. He longs to have you, Christian, talk to Him often. He cares about the details of your life. He will talk to you in the Bible, if you will read it.

Another man, a lawyer, came to Jesus. The record is in Luke 10:25–37. This man asked for help. What does he ask in verse 25? Jesus answers him, but he is not satisfied. How do you know that from verse 29? He tries to make himself look good. Evidently, he didn't really intend to follow the counsel. We do not know what he did.

How about you? Jesus invites you to receive Him as Savior. Have you followed His counsel? He invites you to talk with Him often. Do you? He is the great Counselor. You must follow His direction. Will you be like Nicodemus or the lawyer?

To the Instructor: Make It Visual

You may prepare a role play of two friends talking to each other simultaneously during the opening. Not only will this be humorous, but it will catch attention and focus your topic for today.

Prepare a large placard with the title "Counselor" for your nativity mural (outlined in previous lesson). Explain why this is a Christmas lesson. These are the names of the Baby born to Mary and Joseph. By knowing His names, the students learn more about Him.

Refer to the CEF Biblegram. You will find 11-3, 11-6, 11-7 and 11-8 helpful for visualizing the section of Live It.

HIS NAME IS THE MIGHTY GOD

(Christmas)

Scripture Text: *"For unto us a child is born, unto us a son is given: and the government shall be upon his shoulder: and his name shall be called Wonderful, Counsellor, The mighty God . . ." (Isa. 9:6).*

Lesson Aim: The student will be able to name three names of Jesus from Isaiah 9:6. The student will define "Mighty God" as the strong or able One.

Are You Ready?

Greg tried to move the boulder in the play area. He and his friends, Ted and Brad, wanted to build a fort and the rock was in their way. They tried pushing, pulling, rolling, digging around, and several other ways. The rock hadn't moved an inch. Tired and dirty, the boys took a break at Greg's house for something to eat and a long talk about what to do next.

Greg's dad overheard the boys talking and was amused. He inquired regarding what they had already tried. "Have you done everything you know?" he teased the boys. They were just sure that every possible idea had been thought of and tried. "You haven't asked me," Greg's dad said. "I believe it can be done with the right tools. Let's go have a look."

The boys had exhausted their own resources, but they had forgotten the greater resource of Greg's dad. Have you ever had something so hard to do that you were convinced it was impossible? Have you considered the Lord Jesus' limitless resource and power? He is the Mighty God.

See for Yourself

Quote with me if you can Isaiah 9:6. If you need help, you may open your Bible and read along. What two names for Jesus have we already talked about? He is Wonderful; He is the Counselor. Can you give one reason *why* He is?

The word "mighty" means the able man, the strong one. It means to be strong in yourself, to have an extended sphere of control and to possess binding force. The first definition is easy enough. His power is part of Who Jesus is. He is strong because of Himself. His Person and no one else's effort make Him that way. We will study His extended control as seen in Mark 4:35-41. The binding force can be thought of as the ability to hold things together. Colossians 1:17 states this very clearly. Scientists call this "atomic glue" while we refer to it as the Mighty One Who keeps all His creation from falling apart.

Open your Bible to Mark 4. The disciples had a firsthand demonstration of the Mighty God as seen in Jesus. Read verse 35 to discover the time of day and Jesus' destination. It was evening—probably after dark or getting dark. He wanted to cross the sea to the other side.

Describe the storm in your own words after reading verse 37. The storm was sudden and severe and was quickly submerging the boat they were in. The disciples woke Jesus with fearful words, accusing Him of not caring and allowing them to be killed.

To whom did Jesus speak in verse 39? The wind and the sea were rebuked. This is not unusual because men often talk in anger, frustration, joy and pleasure to the weather. We talk to the rain, the snow, the blazing sun, etc. The unusual thing here is that there was an immediate and complete obedience to

155

Jesus' command. It appeared that His word instantaneously affected the course of the weather.

How did the disciples respond to Jesus' control of the wind and sea? Why did they respond that way? Verse 41 shares their excessive fear. First they feared the storm and then they feared the One Who controlled the storm. As they saw His power to control exercised, they admitted that here was a unique individual. This whole incident added to their conviction that He was more than a man. They had no control over their own fear let alone the danger of the storm; yet this Man, Jesus, controlled the storm and then spoke to quiet their fear, too.

Live It

Jesus, the Mighty God of Mark 4, is desiring to be the Mighty God in your life today. Is He your Savior? Do you as a believer ask for His help daily? He desires to care for you. He is able, strong and mighty. But like Greg and his dad, you must ask for the help of this Son Who was given.

He can work out even the difficult, ugly problems of your life. He is the Mighty God. You must be willing to let Him be Lord. Confession (admitting wrong) and repentance (turning from sin) are necessary as you allow Him to resolve the tangle you have made of your life.

To the Instructor: Make It Visual

You may use flannelgraph figures to visualize the Bible story from Mark 4. Your church or Sunday School may have teaching pictures available. A third option is the CEF Biblegram, "My Wonderful Lord." Visuals 111-3 through 111-7 will do a beautiful job of displaying the story and its progression. Visualize and display the name for Jesus which was studied today (visual shown on facing page).

HIS NAME IS
THE EVERLASTING FATHER
(Christmas)

Scripture Text: *"For unto us a child is born, unto us a son is given: and the government shall be upon his shoulder: and his name shall be called Wonderful, Counsellor, The mighty God, The everlasting Father . . ." (Isa. 9:6).*

Lesson Aim: The student will be able to define "everlasting Father" as the One Who loves, cares, forgives continually. The student should be able to explain how the father of the prodigal son is like the Lord Jesus.

Are You Ready?

It was late Saturday afternoon. Dad had gone to the hardward store with Jeff to get some special tools. Alice looked at Jeff's ten-speed bike longingly. She wanted to go for a ride but she had not asked permission. Dad wasn't home, so how would he ever find out? If she were careful and didn't ride too far, no one would ever know. Alice hopped onto the bike and wheeled her way out into the street. She was being very cautious not to damage Jeff's new bike when she hit a stone, lost control, and down she and the bike fell. She was not hurt, but the reflector over the rear wheel was smashed!

How dumb! Now she would get it. Quickly, Alice

returned to the garage with the bike, parked it and closed the door. Maybe no one would notice. Besides, it was almost time for dinner and Jeff wouldn't be able to ride before Monday. By then Alice would think of something.

Saturday night had never been so long. Sunday dragged on even longer than Alice imagined it ever could. She felt sick about the damage to the bike and even worse about not telling her dad.

Finally, she burst into the room where her dad was reading the newspaper and told the entire tale. Alice cried and said she was sorry. She offered to buy the new reflector that would be needed.

Alice's dad forgave her but agreed that she would have to pay for the new reflector. "Do you still love me?" Alice choked. "Why, yes," replied her dad. "You have been corrected for your wrong but my love for you is just the same."

His name shall be called the Everlasting Father. We will learn today how Jesus is our Father, how His love for us continues on and on.

See for Yourself

Quote with me if you can Isaiah 9:6. You may want to open your Bible and follow along if you are not sure of all the words. What baby boy have we decided that this verse names? Jesus, born in Bethlehem some 700 years after these words were penned by the prophet Isaiah, is the Son Who was given. As He lived and ministered to people, His names seemed to describe His personality truthfully. He was Wonderful, the Counselor, the Mighty God.

Open your Bible to Isaiah 63:16. Isaiah recognizes God as the Father of Israel. Even if Abraham and Jacob will not recognize the Jews, God is their continual Father. His name even tells us that He is a Father that goes on and on. This verse speaks specifically of God, but from Isaiah 9:6 we know that the same relationship is true of the Lord Jesus.

The word "everlasting" means duration, continuity. It carries the concept of an enduring relationship. It outlasts time. The ups and downs of everyday living do not alter His role as our Father. He is the same. He always loves us, cares for us, redeems us, forgives us. You might say He is the "forever Father."

Find Luke 15:11 in your Bible. Here is a parable that Jesus told to some religious men who were upset that Jesus spent time with sinners. This story explains in a beautiful picture how He is the Everlasting Father.

Read verse 11. Who are the characters in the parable? A father and two sons. Evidently the boys lived with their dad and were doing quite well. The family had servants and each boy had a sizable amount of money that would be his at the father's death. The younger son demanded his share of the money. Traveling to a distant place, he wasted this money in careless and sinful living. He spent all that he had been given.

During a famine, the son got a job feeding pigs for a farmer. However, he was hungry himself, so he determined to return home—at least he would have food there. What privileges did the son expect from the father upon his return (vv. 17–19)? None! He realized his sin and honestly felt that he had forfeited the right of being a son. His dad did not have to treat him as a son. How did the father treat the son on his return (vv. 20–24)? The father was waiting and watching and met the boy a good distance from the house. He had compassion on him. He ran as though he were excited to meet him. He hugged him, kissed him, gave him new clothes and shoes and held a banquet. What a picture of the Everlasting Father! He heaps good things on a disobedient, wasteful son.

The son had been wrong. He confessed his sin and asked to be forgiven. The father reinstated him.

Live It

God is the Everlasting Father. He, like the father in Luke 15, is ready to receive you. Have you confessed your sin of rebellion and disobedience to Him? He waits to make you His son. Do it today.

You may be like the son who has gone to a far country. You once received Jesus as Savior and thus God became your Father, but you determined to go your own way. He waits for you to return, also. Why linger in the far country broke, hungry, separated from the Father's care? He longs to have a welcome-home party for you, too. Do it today.

To the Instructor: Make It Visual

A variety of teaching aids may be used to visualize this brief study of the prodigal son and loving father. Flannel-graph, teaching pictures and overhead versions would be useful. Find out what is available and put it to use. The CEF Biblegram, *My Wonderful Lord,* has excellent flashcard illustrations of the Bible story. Pictures IV-3 through IV-6 will prove helpful. There are additional hints and help in the introduction of that series. Add to the Christmas mural today's name for Jesus.

HIS NAME IS PRINCE OF PEACE

(Christmas)

Scripture Text: *"For unto us a child is born, unto us a son is given: and the government shall be upon his shoulder: and his name shall be called Wonderful, Counsellor, The mighty God, The everlasting Father, The Prince of Peace" (Isa. 9:6).*

Lesson Aim: The student will be able to define Prince of Peace as the Captain of peace. The student should determine whether the peace of God rules in his heart.

Are You Ready?

Here are the names of Jesus as they are listed in Isaiah 9:6. As the definition is given, say out loud the name that is described. Ready? The One Who listens, understands and gives advice is _____ (*Counselor*). The One Who is strong and able is _____ (*Mighty God*). The One Who is singular, unique, none like Him is _____ (*Wonderful*). The One Who is forever and loves and cares for His children is _____ (*Everlasting Father*).

Quote with me without the use of your Bible as much of Isaiah 9:6 as you can. "For unto us . . . the Prince of Peace."

What do people worry about? (*Allow several to respond.*) People worry about all sorts of situations, conditions, potential troubles, possible enemies, "maybe's." Why do people worry? (*Engage your pupils in a lively discussion.*) A major reason to worry is concern that something may go wrong. Notice the word "may." Most of our worries are about events yet to come. The past is over; we need not worry about it. The future conceals danger and saps our energy in worry. What do you do when you are worried about something?

Today's lesson centers on the disciples and a particular worry they had. We will learn about the opposite of worry—peace. The last name for the Lord Jesus listed in Isaiah 9:6 is Prince of Peace.

See for Yourself

What is a prince? He is a member of a royal family. His father is the ultimate or highest ruler of the kingdom. The prince enjoys all of the rights and authority associated with the father. He, too, has an important position. The word "prince" in our text means the head, official, captain. As such, the Lord Jesus is the head, the official, the captain of peace. Peace is defined as a restored relationship, completeness. Jesus is the Prince of God. He meets all the requirements of that office.

When Adam sinned, man's relationship with God the Father was broken. There was no peace between God and man. Man was in rebellion, at war with God. Following this idea of a broken relationship, we read, "His name shall be . . . The Prince of Peace." As prince in charge of restoring peace, Jesus came and died, and came to life again after three days. As the risen Lord, He has restored the relationship between God and man. As a man accepts Christ's death for his sin, he makes peace with God. Christ is responsible for the peace between man and God. He is the Peace we enjoy with God.

Later, in Isaiah 26:3, we see how to remain in continuing peace. Read the verse and explain how this can be true. You could read it, "You will keep him in peace whose mind is steady, thinking continually on the Lord." We maintain peace by making the Prince of Peace the focal point of our thoughts.

As trouble and fear enter in, remember the Prince of Peace. Recall His death and victorious resurrection! That will

163

restore your confidence that He is working every event out for your good.

Open your Bible to John 12. We will be looking at a number of places where Jesus tells the disciples and others that He is to die soon. Look at verse 21. What did the Greeks ask? They asked to see Jesus. His answer is in verse 24 and following. What does He say? He is explaining that it is necessary for the Prince to die. If He doesn't die there is no peace for anyone. Jesus was troubled over His death (v. 27), yet determined to accomplish it. Examine verse 33 and tell what is coming for Jesus. His death is clearly told here. Do the people understand (v. 34)? No, they can't figure this out. What clue in verse 35 tells these people that the Prince's death is near? He says, "yet a little while."

Open to chapter 13 and verse 33. What disturbing words does Jesus give to the disciples? They are together with Jesus for a dinner celebration. He is only going to be with them for a short time. They will seek Him after He is gone, He tells them. He is trying to prepare them ahead of time for His departure. Do they understand (v. 36)? No, Peter still wants to know where Jesus is going. Peter is willing and insistent on going with the Lord *now* (v. 37). Does Thomas understand? See John 14:5. No, he is also asking where Jesus is going.

The disciples were worried, troubled, afraid, maybe even frustrated that they could not go with Jesus. In John 14:27 the Prince of Peace gives them what they need. What is it? How were they not to respond?

He gave peace. *His* personal peace made their peace possible. His death and going away made His peace theirs. It was not the world's "patched together" peace (the quiet between conflicts) but the peace of a restored relationship with the Father. They were not to be troubled or afraid. Peace would be theirs!

Live It

Do you have peace? Are you constantly troubled, afraid, worried about something? The Prince of Peace died so you can be at peace with God. Have you accepted His work for you? If you say no, today is the day for you to receive Christ. He will bring to your heart peace with God.

If you say yes, you need to practice Colossians 3:15, "Let the peace of God rule in your hearts. . . ." In other words, you could express it this way: Allow the restored relationship you have with God to umpire, or call the plays, in your life. There will continue to be worrisome and troublesome events in your life as a believer, but you can allow the peace you have before God to dominate and take control of those events. As you are turning your thoughts to the Prince of Peace, His peace will rule in your heart.

To the Instructor: Make It Visual

Select from your picture file a picture of a prince. This will help guide your opening discussion. Pictures of children, youth and adults worrying will be necessary also. You may desire to draw large "worry" and "peace" signs.

Because so much of the lesson comes from the Gospel of John today, you should have extra copies available. Encourage *every* student to enter in. Some will bring their own Bibles; others will need what you provide.

Today is the final lesson in our Christmas series. It would be good to design and make your own Christmas greeting card for each pupil. Copy the mural that you have been using. You could use a mimeograph or a hand-drawn stencil. It will be a greatly appreciated and inexpensive greeting card.